English Grammar for Students of Spanish

The Study Guide
for Those Learning Spanish

Fifth edition

Emily Spinelli
University of Michigan-Dearborn

The Olivia and Hill Press®

ENGLISH GRAMMAR series
Jacqueline Morton, editor

English Grammar for Students of French
English Grammar for Students of German
English Grammar for Students of Italian
English Grammar for Students of Latin
English Grammar for Students of Russian
English Grammar for Students of Japanese
Gramática española para estudiantes de inglés

Printed in the U.S.A.

ISBN: 0-934034-33-8

Library of Congress Control Number: 2002115802

CONTENTS

CONTENTS

CONTENTS

STUDY TIPS

English Grammar for Students of Spanish explains the grammatical terms that are in your Spanish textbook and shows you how they relate to English grammar. Once you understand the terms and concepts in your own language, it will be easier for you to understand what is being introduced in your textbook and by your teacher. To help you become a more efficient language learner, we offer specific *Study Tips* for learning different types of words.

STUDY GUIDE

Before doing an assignment — Read the sections in *English Grammar for Students of Spanish* and in your textbook that cover the topics you are going to study.

Homework — Take notes as you study your textbook. Highlighting is not sufficient. The more often you write down and use vocabulary and rules, the easier it will be for you to remember them. Complete exercises and activities over several short periods of time rather than in one long session.

Written exercises — As you write Spanish words or sentences, say them out loud. Each time you write, read, say, or listen to a word, it reinforces it in your memory.

In class — Take notes. You will know what the teacher considers important and it will reinforce what you are studying.

Objective — You have learned something successfully when you are able to take a blank sheet of paper and write a short sentence in Spanish using the correct form of the Spanish words without reference to a textbook or dictionary. The *Study Tips* below and throughout this handbook will help you with this learning process.

TIPS FOR LEARNING VOCABULARY

One aspect of language learning is remembering a number of foreign words.

To learn vocabulary — Flashcards are a good, handy tool for learning new words and their meaning. You can carry flashcards with you, group them as you wish, and add information as you advance. Creating your own flashcards is an important first step in learning vocabulary.

1. Write the Spanish word or expression on one side of an index card and its English equivalent on the other side.

2. On the Spanish side of the card add a short sentence using the word or expression. It will be easier for you to recall a word in context. To make sure that your sentence is grammatically accurate, copy an example from your textbook. For review purposes, write down the chapter and page number of your textbook where the word is introduced.

3. On the Spanish side, include any irregularities and whatever information is relevant to the word in question. You will find specific suggestions under the *Study Tips* sections of this handbook.

How to use the cards — Regardless of the side of the card you're working on, always say the Spanish word out loud.

1. Look at the Spanish side first. Going from Spanish to English is easier than going from English to Spanish because it only requires your recognizing the Spanish word. Read the Spanish word(s) out loud, giving the English equivalent; then, check your answer on the English side.

2. When you go easily from Spanish to English, turn the cards to the English side. Going from English to Spanish is harder than going from Spanish to English because you have to pull the word and its spelling out of your memory. Say the Spanish equivalent out loud as you write it down on a separate sheet of paper; then check the spelling with the card. Some students prefer closing their eyes and visualizing the Spanish word and its spelling.

3. As you progress, put aside the cards you know and concentrate on the ones you still do not know.

How to remember words — Below are suggestions to help you associate a Spanish word with an English word with a similar meaning. This is the first step and it will put the Spanish word in your short-term memory. Use and practice, the next step, will put the words in your long-term memory.

1. There are many words, called **COGNATES**, that have the same meaning and approximately the same spelling in English as in Spanish. These words are easy to recognize in Spanish, but you will have to concentrate on the differences in spelling and pronunciation.

English	Spanish
important	importante
problem	problema
visit	visitar

2. Try to associate the Spanish word with an English word that has a related meaning.

Spanish	English	Related English word
el avión	*the airplane*	aviation
preocupado	*worried*	preoccupation
el ascensor	*the elevator*	ascend

3. If the Spanish word has no similarities to English, rely on any association that is meaningful to you. The more associations you have for a word, i.e., the more "hooks," the easier it is for you to remember it. Different types of associations work for different people. Find the one that works best for you. Here are some suggestions:

   ■ Group words by topics or personal associations – It is easier to learn new words if you group them. You can group them according to topics such as food, clothing, activities you do for fun, sports, school, home, or according to personal associations such as things you carry in your backpack, things you'd take on a desert island, gifts you'd like to receive, etc.

   ■ Associate the word with an image – If you have trouble remembering a particular word, you might want to create a "bizarre image" in your mind using English words with similar sounds with which to associate it. This method is very subjective and only works for some people.

   > caro = *expensive*
   > You're giving me an *expensive* car 'Oh, boy!'

   > con = *with*
   > "He is a con man *with* charm."

4. To reinforce the Spanish word and its spelling, use it in a short sentence.

Tips for Learning Word Forms

Another aspect of language learning is remembering the various forms a word can take; for example, another form of *book* is *books* and *do* can take the form of *does* and *did*. As a general rule, the first part of the word indicates its meaning and the second part indicates its form.

To learn forms — Paper and pencil are the best tools to learn the various forms of a word. You can write them down until you get them right. The following steps will make learning forms easier.

1. Look for a pattern in the different forms of a word.
   - Which letters, if any, remain constant?
   - Which letters change?
   - Is there a pattern to the changes?
   - Is this pattern the same as one you already know?
   - If this pattern is similar to one you already know, what are the similarities and differences?

   We will help you establish patterns in the *Study Tips* at the end of selected chapters.

2. Once you have established the pattern, it will be easy to memorize the forms.
   - Take a blank piece of paper and write down the forms while saying them out loud.
   - Continue until you are able to write all the forms correctly without referring to your textbook.

3. Write short sentences using the various forms.

To review forms — You can use flashcards to review forms, not to learn them. You will find suggestions on what to write on the cards under the *Study Tips* of selected chapters listed in the Table of Contents.[1]

---

[1]We wish to thank Hélène Neu of the University of Michigan, Ann Arbor, for her valuable contributions to the *Study Tips*.

CHAPTER

WHAT'S IN A WORD?

When you learn a foreign language, in this case Spanish, [1]
you must look at each word in four ways:
MEANING, PART OF SPEECH, FUNCTION and FORM.

MEANING

An English word may be connected to a Spanish word
that has a similar meaning.

> *House*, a building in which people live, has the same mean-
> ing as the Spanish word **casa**.

Words with equivalent meanings are learned by memo- [10]
rizing VOCABULARY (see pp. 1-3).
Occasionally knowing one Spanish word will help you
learn another.

> Knowing that **niño** means *boy* should help you learn that
> **niña** is *girl*; or knowing that **hermano** is *brother* should
> help you remember that **hermana** is *sister*.

Usually, however, there is little similarity between words
and knowing one Spanish word will not help you learn
another. As a general rule, you must memorize each [20]
vocabulary item separately.

> Knowing that **hombre** is *man* will not help you learn that
> **mujer** is *woman*.

In addition, every language has expressions in which
the meaning of a group of words is different from the
meaning of the words taken individually. These are called
IDIOMATIC EXPRESSIONS, or IDIOMS. For instance, *"to fall*
asleep" and *"to take* a walk" are English expressions where
"to fall" and *"to take"* do not have their usual meaning as [30]
in *"to fall* down the stairs," or *"to take* a book to school."
You will have to be on the alert for these idioms because
they cannot be translated word-for-word in Spanish.

> *to fall asleep*   dormirse
> [word-for-word *"to put oneself to sleep"*]
>
> *to take a walk*   dar un paseo
> [word-for-word *"to give a walk"*]

PART OF SPEECH

In English and Spanish words are grouped according to how they are used in a sentence. There are eight groups corresponding to eight PARTS OF SPEECH:

adjectives	nouns
adverbs	pronouns
articles	prepositions
conjunctions	verbs

Some parts of speech are further broken down according to type. Adjectives, for instance, can be descriptive, interrogative, demonstrative, or possessive. Each part of speech has its own rules for spelling, pronunciation, and use.

In order to choose the correct Spanish equivalent of an English word, you will have to identify its part of speech. As an example, look at the word *leaves* in the following two sentences. In each sentence *leaves* belongs to a different part of speech, each one corresponding to a different Spanish word.

John *leaves* the room.

verb = **sale**

John swept the *leaves* off the deck.

noun = **hojas**

The various sections of this handbook show you how to identify parts of speech so that you are able to choose the proper Spanish words and the rules that apply to them.

FUNCTION

In English and Spanish the role a word plays in a sentence is called its FUNCTION. For example, words that are nouns can have the following functions:

subject
direct object
indirect object
object of a preposition

In order to choose the correct Spanish equivalent of an English word, you will have to identify its function. As an example, look at the word *him* in the following two sentences. In each sentence *him* has a different function, each one corresponding to a different Spanish word.

They don't see *him*.

direct object = **lo**

I wrote *him* a letter.
80
    |
  indirect object = **le**

The various sections of this handbook show you how to identify the function of words so that you are able to choose the proper Spanish words and the rules that apply to them.

FORM

In English and in Spanish, a word can influence the form of another word, that is, its spelling and pronunciation. This "matching" is called AGREEMENT and it is said that one word "agrees" with another.
90

   I am   *am* agrees with *I*
   she is   *is* agrees with *she*

Agreement does not play a big role in English, but it is an important part of the Spanish language. As an example, look at the sentences below where the lines indicate which words must agree with one another.

   *My older **brother** works in that large modern **office**.*
   |_____|
   Mi **hermano** mayor trabaja en esa **oficina** grande y moderna.
100
   |___| |_____| |___| |_____|

In English, the only word that affects another word in the sentence is *brother*, which forces us to say *works*. If we changed *brother* to *brothers*, we would have to say *work* to make it agree with *brothers*.

In Spanish, the word for *brother* (**hermano**) not only affects the spelling and pronunciation of *works* (**trabaja**), but also the spelling and pronunciation of the Spanish words for *my* (**mi**) and *older* (**mayor**). The word for *office* (**oficina**) affects the spelling and pronunciation of the
110
Spanish words for *that* (**esa**), *large* (**grande**), and *modern* (**moderna**). If we changed *brother* to *sister* and *office* to *offices* all the affected words would also have to change.

As the various parts of speech are introduced in this handbook, we will go over "agreement" so that you learn which words agree with others and how the agreement is shown.

WHAT IS A NOUN?

A **NOUN** is a word that can be the name of
a person, animal, place, thing, event or idea.

- **a person**   professor, clown, student, girl, baby
  Professor Smith, Bozo, Bill, Mary
- **an animal**   elephant, horse, snake, eagle
  Kermit, Bambi, Garfield, Teddy
- **a place**   stadium, restaurant, city, state, country
  Madrid, Michigan, Mexico, South America
- **a thing**   apple, lamp, dress, airplane
  Coca-Cola, the White House, a Cadillac
- **an event**   graduation, marriage, birth, Thanksgiving
  or activity   the Olympics, shopping, rest, growth
- **an idea**   democracy, humor, hatred, honor
  or concept   time, love, justice, jealousy, poverty

As you can see, a noun is not only a word that names
something that is tangible (i.e., something you can
touch), such as a *lamp, horse,* or *White House,* it can also be
the name of things that are abstract (i.e., that you cannot
touch), such as *justice, jealousy,* and *honor.*

A noun that does not state the name of a specific person, place, thing, etc. is called a **COMMON NOUN.** A common noun does not begin with a capital letter, unless it is
the first word of a sentence. All the nouns above that are
not capitalized are common nouns.

A noun that is the name of a specific person, place,
thing, etc. is called a **PROPER NOUN.** A proper noun always
begins with a capital letter. All the nouns above that are
capitalized are proper nouns.

> Bill is my friend.
> proper   common
> noun   noun

A noun that is made up of two words is called a **COM-
POUND NOUN.** A compound noun can be composed of two
common nouns, such as *comic strip* and *ice cream,* or two
proper nouns, such as *South America* or *Mexico City.*

IN ENGLISH

To help you learn to recognize nouns, look at the paragraph below where the nouns are in *italics*.

> The *countries* that make up the Spanish-speaking *world* export *products* that we use every *day*. *Spain* produces many of the *shoes, purses,* and *gloves* that are sold in *stores* throughout the *United States*. *Spain* also sells us much *wine, sherry,* and *brandy*. The *islands* of the *Caribbean* and the *nations* of *Central America* supply us with tropical *fruits* such as *bananas* and *melons; sugar* is another important *export* of these *regions*. While *oil* is a major *source* of *income* for *Mexico* and *Venezuela*, the *economies* of several other *countries* of *Latin America* depend upon the *production* and *exportation* of *coffee*.

40
50

IN SPANISH

Nouns are identified in the same way as they are in English.

TERMS USED TO TALK ABOUT NOUNS

- **GENDER** — A noun has a gender; that is, it can be classified according to whether it is masculine, feminine, or neuter (see *What is Meant by Gender?*, p. 10).
- **NUMBER** — A noun has a number; that is, it can be identified according to whether it is singular or plural (see *What is Meant by Number?*, p. 14).
- **FUNCTION** — A noun can have a variety of functions in a sentence; that is, it can be the subject of the sentence (see *What is a Subject?*, p. 29) or an object (see *What are Objects?*, p. 140).

60

✎ REVIEW

Circle the nouns in the following sentences:

1. Students came into the classroom and spoke to the teacher.

2. The Wilsons went on a tour of Mexico.

3. Figure skating is an exciting event in the Winter Olympics.

4. Buenos Aires, the capital of Argentina, is a cosmopolitan city.

5. Truth is stranger than fiction.

6. They want a boss with intelligence and a sense of humor.

STUDY TIPS — NOUNS (SEE P. 19)

CHAPTER

WHAT IS MEANT BY GENDER?

GENDER in the grammatical sense means that a word can be classified as masculine, feminine, or neuter.

> Did Paul give Mary the book?
> Yes, *he* gave *it* to *her.*
>   masc.   neuter fem.

Grammatical gender is not very important in English; however, it is at the very heart of the Spanish language where the gender of a word is often reflected not only in the way the word itself is spelled and pronounced, but also in the way all the words connected to it are spelled and pronounced.

More parts of speech have a gender in Spanish than in English.

ENGLISH	SPANISH
pronouns	pronouns
possessive adjectives	adjectives
	articles
	nouns

Since each part of speech follows its own rules to indicate gender, you will find gender discussed in the chapters dealing with articles and the various types of pronouns and adjectives. In this section we shall only look at the gender of nouns.

IN ENGLISH

Nouns themselves do not have a gender, but sometimes their meaning will indicate a gender based on the biological sex of the person or animal the noun stands for. For example, when we replace a proper or common noun which refers to a man or a woman, we use *he* for males and *she* for females.

- nouns referring to males indicate the **MASCULINE** gender

  Paul came home; *he* was tired, and I was glad to see *him.*
      noun (male)   masculine   masculine

- nouns referring to females indicate the **FEMININE** gender

  Mary came home; *she* was tired, and I was glad to see *her.*
      noun (female)   feminine   feminine

All the proper or common nouns that do not have a biological gender are considered **NEUTER** and are replaced by *it*.   40

> The city of Washington is lovely. I enjoyed visiting *it*.
>   noun   neuter

IN SPANISH

All nouns — common nouns and proper nouns — have a gender; they are either masculine or feminine. Do not confuse the grammatical terms "masculine" and "feminine" with the terms "male" and "female." Only a few Spanish nouns have a grammatical gender tied to whether they refer to someone of the male or female sex, most nouns have a gender which must be memorized.   50

The gender of common and proper nouns based on **BIOLOGICAL GENDER** is easy to determine. These are nouns whose meaning can only refer to one or the other of the biological sexes, male or female.

MALES → MASCULINE	FEMALES → FEMININE
Paul	Mary
boy	girl
brother	sister
stepfather	niece

60

The gender of all other nouns, common and proper, cannot be explained or figured out. These nouns have a **GRAMMATICAL GENDER** that is unrelated to biological gender and which must be memorized. Here are some examples of English nouns classified under the gender of their Spanish equivalent.

MASCULINE	FEMININE
money	coin
dress	shirt
country	nation
Peru	Argentina
Wednesday	peace

70

As you learn a new noun, you should always learn its gender because it will affect the spelling and pronunciation of the words related to it. Textbooks and dictionaries usually indicate the gender of a noun with an *m.* for masculine or an *f.* for feminine. Sometimes the definite articles are used: **el** for masculine or **la** for feminine (see *What are Articles?*, p. 16).   80

ENDINGS INDICATING GENDER

Gender can sometimes be determined by looking at the end of the Spanish noun. In the lists that follow there are endings that often indicate feminine nouns and others that indicate masculine nouns. Since you will encounter many nouns with these endings in basic Spanish, it is certainly worthwhile to familiarize yourself with them.

FEMININE ENDINGS

-a	la casa, la biblioteca	*house, library*
-dad, **-tad**	la ciu**dad**, la liber**tad**	*city, liberty*
-z	la nariz	*nose*
-ión, **-ción**	la reun**ión**, la na**ción**	*meeting, nation*
-umbre	la cost**umbre**	*custom*
-ie	la espec**ie**	*species*

MASCULINE ENDINGS

Any ending except those provided in the "Feminine endings" list above. In particular:

-l	el pape**l**	*paper*
-o	el libr**o**	*book*
-n	el jardí**n**	*garden*
-e	el parqu**e**	*park*
-r	el dolo**r**	*pain*
-s	el interé**s**	*interest*

To help you remember these endings note that for the masculine endings the letters spell "loners."

There are, of course, exceptions to the above rules. For instance, **mano** *(hand)* is a feminine word even though it ends with the letter **-o** and **día** *(day)* is a masculine word even though it ends with the letter **-a.** Your textbook and instructor will point out the exceptions that you will need to learn.

CAREFUL — Do not rely on biological gender to indicate the grammatical gender of Spanish equivalents of nouns that can refer to a man or a woman. For instance, the grammatical gender of the noun **"persona"** *(person)* is always feminine, even though the person being referred to could be a man or a woman.

90

100

110

✎ REVIEW

Circle M (masculine) or F (feminine) next to the nouns whose gender you can identify, and (?) next to the nouns whose gender you would have to look up in a dictionary.

GENDER IN SPANISH

1. boys	M	F	?
2. chair	M	F	?
3. Cathy	M	F	?
4. classroom	M	F	?
5. visitor	M	F	?
6. sisters	M	F	?
7. blouses	M	F	?

STUDY TIPS — NOUNS (SEE P. 19)

WHAT IS MEANT BY NUMBER?

NUMBER in the grammatical sense means that a word can be classified as singular or plural. When a word refers to one person or thing, it is said to be **SINGULAR;** when it refers to more than one, it is **PLURAL.**

one *book*   two *books*
singular   plural

More parts of speech indicate number in Spanish than in English and there are also more spelling and pronunciation changes in Spanish than in English.

ENGLISH	SPANISH
nouns	nouns
verbs	verbs
pronouns	pronouns
demonstrative adjectives	adjectives
	articles

Since each part of speech follows its own rules to indicate number, you will find number discussed in the sections dealing with articles, the various types of adjectives and pronouns, as well as in all the sections on verbs. In this section we shall only look at the number of nouns.

IN ENGLISH

A singular noun is made plural in one of two ways:

1. a singular noun can add an *"-s"* or *"-es"*

book   book*s*
church   church*es*

2. other singular nouns change their spelling

man   men
mouse   mice
leaf   leaves
child   children

Some nouns, called **COLLECTIVE NOUNS**, refer to a group of persons or things, but the noun itself is considered singular.

A football *team* has eleven players.
My *family* is well.

IN SPANISH

As in English, the plural form of a noun is usually spelled differently from the singular. 40

1. The most common change is the same as the one made in English; that is, an "-s" is added to singular masculine or feminine nouns that end in a vowel.

	SINGULAR	PLURAL		
MASCULINE	libro	libros	*book*	*books*
FEMININE	mesa	mesas	*table*	*tables*

2. Nouns that end in a consonant add "-es" to form a plural.

50

	SINGULAR	PLURAL		
MASCULINE	papel	papeles	*paper*	*papers*
FEMININE	ciudad	ciudades	*city*	*cities*

A few nouns will have internal spelling changes when they become plural. Your instructor and textbook will point out the exceptions to the two basic rules listed above.

✎ REVIEW

Look at the English and Spanish words below. Indicate if the word is singular (S) or plural (P).

1. teeth   S   P

2. family   S   P

3. dress   S   P

4. mice   S   P

5. **coches**   S   P

6. **mujer**   S   P

WHAT ARE ARTICLES?

An ARTICLE is a word placed before a noun to show whether the noun refers to a specific person, animal, place, thing, event, or idea, or whether it refers to a non-specific person, thing, or idea.

> I saw *the* boy you spoke about.
> |
> a specific boy

> I saw *a* boy in the street.
> |
> not a specific boy

In English and in Spanish there are two types of articles, DEFINITE ARTICLES and INDEFINITE ARTICLES.

DEFINITE ARTICLES

IN ENGLISH

A DEFINITE ARTICLE is used before a noun when we are speaking about a specific person, place, animal, thing, or idea. There is one definite article, ***the***.

> I read *the* book you recommended.
> |
> a specific book

> I ate *the* apple you gave me.
> |
> a specific apple

The definite article remains *the* even when the noun that follows becomes plural.

> I read *the books* you recommended.
> I ate *the apples* you gave me.

IN SPANISH

As in English, a definite article is used before a noun when referring to a specific person, place, animal, thing, or idea.

> Comí **la** manzana que me diste.
> *I ate **the** apple you gave me.*

In Spanish, the definite article is also used when speaking in general terms.

Me gustan **los gatos** pero odio **los perros.**
I like cats [in general] but I hate dogs [in general].

Los perros son más fieles que **los gatos.**
Dogs are more faithful than cats.

In Spanish, the article works hand-in-hand with the noun to which it belongs in that it matches the noun's gender and number. This "matching" is called AGREEMENT. One says that "the article *agrees* with the noun." (See *What is Meant by Gender?*, p. 10 and *What is Meant by Number?*, p. 14.)

A different article is used, therefore, depending on whether the noun is masculine or feminine (gender) and depending on whether the noun is singular or plural (number).

There are four forms of the definite article: two singular forms and two plural forms.

- **el** indicates that the noun is masculine singular

    el libro   *the book*
    el muchacho   *the boy*

- **la** indicates that the noun is feminine singular

    la casa   *the house*
    la muchacha   *the girl*

- **los** indicates that the noun is masculine plural

    los libros   *the books*
    los muchachos *the boys*

- **las** indicates that the noun is feminine plural

    las casas   *the houses*
    las muchachas *the girls*

Memorize nouns with the singular definite article; in most cases the article will tell you if the noun is masculine or feminine.[1]

---

[1]There are only a few exceptions to this statement. The primary exceptions are those feminine nouns that begin with a stressed **a-** and which for pronunciation purposes take **el** as the article: **el agua, el águila.** The noun is nonetheless still feminine: **el agua fría.**

INDEFINITE ARTICLES

IN ENGLISH

An **INDEFINITE ARTICLE** is used before a noun when we are not speaking about a specific person, animal, place, thing, event, or idea. There are two indefinite articles, *a* and *an*.

- *a* is used before a word beginning with a consonant[1]

  I saw *a* boy in the street.
  |
  not a specific boy

- *an* is used before a word beginning with a vowel

  I ate *an* apple.
  |
  not a specific apple

The indefinite article is used only with a singular noun. To indicate a nonspecific plural noun, the word *some* can be used, but it is usually left out.

  I saw boys in the street.
  I saw *(some)* boys in the street.

  I ate apples.
  I ate *(some)* apples.

IN SPANISH

As in English, an indefinite article is used before a noun when we are not speaking about a specific person, animal, place, thing, event, or idea.

Just as with definite articles, indefinite articles must agree with the noun's gender and number.

There are four forms of the indefinite article: two singular forms and two plural forms.

- **un** indicates that the noun is masculine singular

  | **un** libro | *a book* |
  | **un** muchacho | *a boy* |

- **una** indicates that the noun is feminine singular

  | **una** casa | *a house* |
  | **una** muchacha | *a girl* |

- **unos** indicates that the noun is masculine plural

  | **unos** libros | *(some)* books |
  | **unos** muchachos | *(some)* boys |

---

[1]Vowels are the sounds associated with the letters *a, e, i, o, u* and sometimes *y*; consonants are the sounds associated with the other letters of the alphabet.

- **unas** indicates that the noun is feminine plural

unas casas	*(some) houses*
unas muchachas	*(some) girls*

Your textbook will instruct you on additional uses of the definite and indefinite articles in Spanish.

CAREFUL — Unlike English where a noun can be used without an article (*Truth* is stranger than *fiction*; *Mexico* is a beautiful *country*), Spanish common and proper nouns are usually preceded by an article: definite or indefinite.

120

✎ REVIEW

Below is a list of English nouns preceded by a definite or indefinite article.

- Write the Spanish article for each noun on the line provided. The Spanish dictionary entry shows you if the noun (n.) is masculine (m.) or feminine (f.).

	DICTIONARY ENTRY	SPANISH ARTICLE
1. the books	**libro** (n. m.)	_____
2. a table	**mesa** (n. f.)	_____
3. some classes	**clase** (n. f.)	_____
4. the telephone	**teléfono** (n. m.)	_____
5. a car	**coche** (n. m.)	_____
6. the sisters	**hermana** (n. f.)	_____
7. some men	**hombre** (n. m.)	_____
8. an apple	**manzana** (n. f.)	_____
9. the ball	**pelota** (n. f.)	_____

STUDY TIPS — NOUNS AND THEIR GENDER

Flashcards (see *Tips for Learning Vocabulary*, pp. 1-3)

1. Make a flashcard for each new noun. On the Spanish side, list the singular form; list the plural form only if it is irregular.
2. Use blue cards or blue ink for masculine nouns and red cards or red ink for feminine nouns.
3. Precede the noun with the appropriate definite article: **el** or **la**.

Pattern

1. Memorize the noun endings that indicate gender (see p. 12). Make sure that you memorize a sample word for each ending.

2. As you learn a new noun, look at its ending to see if the above list applies. If it does, the noun's gender will be easier to remember.

Practice

1. Whether you're looking at the Spanish or the English side of the card, as you say the Spanish noun and article, add a word such as "nuevo" (*new*) whose ending changes according to whether it accompanies a masculine or feminine noun (with a masculine noun the form is **nuevo**; with a feminine noun the form is **nueva**). The change in the form of the word will help reinforce the noun's gender in your memory.

el libro (nuevo)	*the (new) book*
la casa (nueva)	*the (new) house*

2. Don't forget that it is only by repeated use that you will remember the words and their gender.

WHAT IS THE POSSESSIVE?

The term **POSSESSIVE** means that one noun owns or *possesses* another noun. 1

Mary*'s* Spanish book is on the table.
| |
possessor   possessed

IN ENGLISH

There are two constructions to show possession.

1. An apostrophe can be used. In this construction, the possessor comes before the possessed.

- singular possessor adds an apostrophe + "s" 10

  > Mary*'s* dress
  > a tree*'s* branches
  > |
  > singular possessor

- plural possessor ending with "s" adds an apostrophe after the "s"

  > the students*'* teacher
  > the girls*'* club
  > |
  > plural possessor

 20

- plural possessor not ending with "s" adds an apostrophe + "s"

  > the children*'s* playground
  > the men*'s* department
  > |
  > plural possessor

2. The word *of* can be used. In this structure, the possessed comes before the possessor.

- a singular or plural possessor is preceded by *of the* or *of a*

 30

  > the book *of the* professor
  > the branches *of a* tree
  > |
  > singular possessor

  > the teacher *of the* students
  > |
  > plural possessor

IN SPANISH

There is only one way to express possession and that is by using the "of" construction (No. 2 above). The apostrophe structure (No. 1 above) does not exist.

The Spanish structure parallels the English structure: the noun possessed + **de** ("of") + definite or indefinite article + the noun possessor (if the noun possessor is a proper noun, there is no preceding article).

Mary's dress	el vestido **de** María
| |	| |
possessor possessed	possessed possessor
	the dress of Mary
the professor's book	el libro **del** profesor
	|
	de + el
	the book of the professor
the woman's purse	la bolsa **de la** señora
	the purse of the woman
a tree's branches	las ramas **de un** árbol
	the branches of a tree
the girls' father	el padre **de las** muchachas
	the father of the girls
the boys' team	el equipo **de los** muchachos
	the team of the boys

✎ **REVIEW**

Below are possessives using the apostrophe. Write the alternate English structure that is the word-for-word equivalent of the Spanish structure.

1. some children's parents

_____

2. the doctor's office

_____

3. a car's headlights

_____

4. the girls' soccer coach

_____

5. Gloria Smith's mother

_____

WHAT IS A VERB?

A **VERB** is a word that indicates the action of the sentence. The word "action" is used in the broadest sense, not necessarily physical action.

Let us look at different types of words that are verbs:

- a physical activity   to run, to hit, to talk, to walk
- a mental activity   to hope, to believe, to imagine, to dream, to think
- a condition   to be, to feel, to have, to seem

Many verbs, however, do not fall neatly into one of the above three categories. They are verbs nevertheless because they represent the "action" of the sentence.

The book *costs* only $5.00.
|
to cost

The students *seem* tired.
|
to seem

The verb is the most important word in a sentence. You cannot write a **COMPLETE SENTENCE**, that is, express a complete thought, without a verb.

It is important to identify verbs because the function of the other words in a sentence often depends on their relationship to the verb. For instance, the subject of a sentence is the word doing the action of the verb, and the object is the word receiving the action of the verb (see *What is a Subject?*, p. 29, and *What are Objects?*, p. 140).

IN ENGLISH

To help you learn to recognize verbs, look at the paragraph below where the verbs are in italics.

The three students *entered* the restaurant, *selected* a table, *hung* up their coats and *sat* down. They *looked* at the menu and *asked* the waitress what she *recommended*. She *advised* the daily special, beef stew. It *was* not expensive. They *chose* a bottle of red wine and *ordered* a salad. The service *was* slow, but the food *tasted* very good. Good cooking, they *decided*, *takes* time. They *ate* pastry for dessert and *finished* the meal with coffee.

IN SPANISH

Verbs are identified the same way as they are in English.

TERMS TO TALK ABOUT VERBS

- INFINITIVE OR DICTIONARY FORM — The verb form that is the name of the verb is called an infinitive: *to eat, to sleep, to drink* (see *What is the Infinitive?*, p. 25). In the dictionary a verb is listed without the "to": *eat, sleep, drink*.

- CONJUGATION — A verb is conjugated or changes in form to agree with its subject: *I do, he does* (see *What is a Verb Conjugation?*, p. 41).

- TENSE — A verb indicates tense, that is, the time (present, past, or future) of the action: *I am, I was, I will be* (see *What is Meant by Tense?*, p. 64).

- MOOD — A verb shows mood, that is the speaker's attitude toward what he or she is saying (see *What is Meant by Mood?*, p. 79).

- VOICE — A verb shows voice, that is, the relation between the subject and the action of the verb (see *What is Meant by Active and Passive Voice?*, p. 104).

- PARTICIPLE — A verb may be used to form a participle: *writing, written; singing, sung* (see *What is a Participle?*, p. 73).

- TRANSITIVE OR INTRANSITIVE — A verb can be classified as transitive or intransitive depending on whether or not the verb can take a direct object (see *What are Objects?*, p. 140).

✎ **REVIEW**

Circle the verbs in the following sentences.

1. The students purchase their lunch at school.

2. Paul and Mary were happy.

3. They enjoyed the movie, but they preferred the book.

4. Paul ate dinner, finished his novel, and then went to bed.

5. It was sad to see the little dog struggle to get out of the lake.

6. I attended a concert to celebrate the New Year.

STUDY TIPS — VERBS (SEE P. 27)

WHAT IS THE INFINITIVE?

The **INFINITIVE** form is the name of the verb.
The Spanish equivalent of the verb *to study* is **estudiar**.
infinitive

IN ENGLISH

The infinitive is composed of two words: *to* + the **DICTIO-
NARY FORM** of the verb *(to speak, to dance)*. By infinitive we
mean the form of the verb that is listed as the entry in the
dictionary *(speak, dance)*.

Although the infinitive is the most basic form of the
verb, it can never be used in a sentence without another
verb that is conjugated (see *What is a Verb Conjugation?*,
p. 41).

>*To learn is* exciting.
>infinitive conjugated verb

>It *is* important *to be* on time.
>conjugated verb infinitive

>Paul and Mary *want to dance* together.
>conjugated verb infinitive

The dictionary form of the verb, rather than the infinitive, is used after such verbs as *let, must, should,* and *can.*

>Mr. Smith *let* his daughter *drive* his new car.
>dictionary form

>Paul *must be* home by noon.
>dictionary form

IN SPANISH

The infinitive form is composed of only one word. The
word *to* that is part of the English infinitive has no
Spanish equivalent. The Spanish infinitive is identified by
the last two letters of the verb called **THE ENDING.**

>hablar   *to speak*
>comer   *to eat*
>vivir   *to live*

The infinitive form is important not only because it is the form under which a verb is listed in the dictionary, but also because the ending indicates the pattern the verb will follow to create its various forms.

1ˢᵀ CONJUGATION — verbs ending in **-ar** follow one pattern

2ᴺᴰ CONJUGATION — verbs ending in -**er** follow another pattern

3ᴿᴰ CONJUGATION — verbs ending in **-ir** follow another pattern

In a sentence the infinitive form is always used for a verb that follows any verb other than **ser** *(to be)*, **estar** *(to be)*, or **haber** *(to have)*.

> *John and Mary want **to dance** together.*
> Juan y María quieren **bailar** juntos.
> |
>   infinitive

> *I can **leave** tomorrow.*
> Puedo **salir** mañana.
> |
>   infinitive

> *You should **study** more.*
> Usted debe **estudiar** más.
> |
>   infinitive

Notice that in the last two examples there is no "to" in the English sentence to alert you that an infinitive must be used in Spanish.

CAREFUL — You cannot depend upon the English sentence to alert you to the use of the infinitive in Spanish. Often the word "to" will not be used in the English sentence but the infinitive must be used in Spanish.

CONSULTING THE DICTIONARY

In English it is possible to change the meaning of a verb by placing short words (prepositions or adverbs) after it.

For example, the verb *look* in Column A below changes meaning depending on the word that follows it *(to, after, for, into)*. In Spanish it is not generally possible to change the meaning of a verb by adding a preposition or an adverb as in Column A. An entirely different Spanish verb corresponds to each meaning.

COLUMN A		MEANING	SPANISH
to look	→	to look at	**mirar**
		I *looked at* the photo.	
to look for	→	to search for	**buscar**
		I *am looking for* my book.	

to look after → to take care of   **cuidar**
                    I *am looking after* the children.

to look into   → to study   **estudiar**
                    We*'ll look into* the problem.

When consulting an English-Spanish dictionary, all the examples above under Column A can be found under the dictionary entry *look* (**mirar**); however, you will have to search under that entry for the specific expression *look for* (**buscar**) or *look after* (**cuidar**) to find the correct Spanish equivalent.

Don't select the first entry under *look* and then add on the Spanish equivalent for *after, for, into*, etc.; the result will be meaningless in Spanish.

✎ REVIEW

Circle the words that you would replace with an infinitive in Spanish.

1. Mary has nothing more to do today.

2. You must study your lesson.

3. Jeff wants to learn Spanish.

4. They cannot leave on Tuesday.

5. We hope to travel through Spain this summer.

STUDY TIPS — VERBS

Flashcards (see *Tips for Learning Vocabulary*, pp. 1-3)

1. Create flashcards indicating the infinitive form of the Spanish verb on one side and its English equivalent on the other.

   aprender   *to learn*

   You might want to select a particular color for verb cards so that later when you add information on the cards you can easily sort them out from the other cards (see *Study Tips — Verb Conjugations*, p. 48; *Tenses,* p. 66; *The Preterite*, p. 72; *The Future Tense*, p. 97).

2. If the verb is a reflexive verb, indicate "se" at the end of the infinitive (see *What are Reflexive Pronouns and Verbs?*, p. 161). If the verb can be used as a reflexive verb and as a non-reflexive verb, write both forms with examples.

   poner   to put
   Juan **pone** los libros en su mochila.   *John **puts** the books in his backpack.*

   ponerse   to put on
   Juan **se pone** los zapatos.   *John **puts on** his shoes.*

3. If the verb is followed by a preposition such as "de" or can be part of a special construction, indicate it on the card with an example.

salir **de**	*to leave*
Salimos de la casa a las ocho.	*We leave the house at eight.*
tener **(que** + infinitive)	*to have to + do something*
Tenemos que estudiar mucho.	*We have to study a lot.*

Practice

Follow the *Tips for Learning Vocabulary*, pp. 1-3 to learn the Spanish equivalent of English verbs. The real practice will come, however, when you learn to conjugate the verb and to use the conjugated forms in sentences.

WHAT IS A SUBJECT?

In a sentence the person or thing that performs the action of the verb is called the SUBJECT.

To find the subject of a sentence, always look for the verb first; then ask, *who?* or *what?* before the verb (see *What is a Verb?*, p. 23). The answer will be the subject.[1]

> Teresa speaks Spanish.
>> VERB: speaks
>> Who speaks Spanish? ANSWER: Teresa.
>> The subject refers to one person; it is singular (see p. 14).

> Teresa's books cost a lot of money.
>> VERB: cost
>> What costs a lot of money? ANSWER: books.
>> The subject refers to more than one thing; it is plural (p. 14).

If a verb has more than one subject, the subject is considered plural.

> The book and the pencil are on the table.
>> VERB: are
>> What is on the table? ANSWER: the book and the pencil.
>> The subject refers to more than one thing; it is plural.

If a sentence has more than one verb, you have to find the subject of each verb.

> The boys were cooking while Mary set the table.
>> *Boys* is the plural subject of *were.*
>> *Mary* is the singular subject of *set.*

IN ENGLISH

Always ask *who?* or *what?* before the verb to find the subject. Never assume that the first word in the sentence is the subject. Subjects can be located in several different places, as you can see in the following examples (the subject is in **boldface** and the verb is *italicized*):

> *Did* **the game** *start* on time?
> After playing for two hours, **Paul** *became* exhausted.
> Mary's **brothers** *arrived* yesterday.

---

[1]The subject performs the action in an active sentence, but is acted upon in a passive sentence (see *What is Meant by Active and Passive Voice?*, p. 104).

IN SPANISH

The subject of a sentence is identified the same way as it is in English. Also, as in English, it can be located in different places in the sentence.

40

CAREFUL — In both English and Spanish it is important to find the subject of each verb to make sure that the verb form agrees with the subject (see *What is a Verb Conjugation?*, p. 41).

✎ **REVIEW**

Find the subjects in the sentences below.
- Next to Q, write the question you need to ask to find the subject of the sentences below.
- Next to A, write the answer to the question you just asked.
- Circle if the subject is singular (S) or plural (P).

1. When the bell rang, all the children ran out.

    Q: _____

    A: _____   S   P

    Q: _____

    A: _____   S   P

2. One waiter took the order and another brought the food.

    Q: _____

    A: _____   S   P

    Q: _____

    A: _____   S   P

3. The first-year students voted for the class president.

    Q: _____

    A: _____   S   P

4. They say that Spanish is a beautiful language.

    Q: _____

    A: _____   S   P

    Q: _____

    A: _____   S   P

WHAT IS A PRONOUN?

A **PRONOUN** is a word used in place of one or more nouns. It may stand, therefore, for a person, animal, place, thing, event, or idea.

For instance, rather than repeating the proper noun "Paul" in the following sentences, "Paul" can be replaced by a pronoun in the second sentence.

> Paul likes to swim. Paul practices every day.
> Paul likes to swim. *He* practices every day.

A pronoun can only be used to refer to someone (or something) that has already been mentioned. The word that the pronoun replaces or refers to is called the **ANTECEDENT** of the pronoun. In the example above, the pronoun *he* refers to the proper noun *Paul*. *Paul* is the antecedent of the pronoun *he*.

There are different types of pronouns, each serves a different function and follows different rules. Listed below are the more important types and the chapters in which they are discussed.

PERSONAL PRONOUNS — These pronouns replace nouns referring to persons or things that have been previously mentioned. A different set of pronouns is often used depending on the pronoun's function in the sentence.

- subject (see p. 33)
  > *I* go; *they* read; *he* runs; *she* sings.

- direct object pronouns (see p. 147)
  > John loves *her*. Jane saw *him* at the theater.

- indirect object pronouns (see p. 147)
  > John gave *us* the book. My mother wrote *me* a letter.

- object of preposition pronouns (p. 156)
  > Robert is going to the movies with *us*.

REFLEXIVE PRONOUNS — These pronouns refer back to the subject of the sentence (see p. 161).

> I cut *myself*. We washed *ourselves*. Mary dressed *herself*.

INTERROGATIVE PRONOUNS — These pronouns are used to ask questions (see p. 172).

> *Who* is that? *What* do you want?

DEMONSTRATIVE PRONOUNS — These pronouns are used to point out persons or things (see p. 180).

> *This (one)* is expensive. *That (one)* is cheap.

POSSESSIVE PRONOUNS — These pronouns are used to show possession or ownership (see p. 166).

> Whose book is that? *Mine. Yours* is on the table.

RELATIVE PRONOUNS — These pronouns are used to introduce relative subordinate clauses (see p. 184).

> The man *who* just walked in is my instructor.
> This is the sweater *that* I bought last week.

INDEFINITE PRONOUNS — These pronouns are used to refer to unidentified persons or things (see p. 195).

> *One* should not do that.
> *Something* is wrong.

Spanish indefinite pronouns correspond in usage to their English equivalents. They can be studied in your textbook.

IN ENGLISH

Each type of pronoun follows a different set of rules.

IN SPANISH

As in English, each type of pronoun follows a different set of rules. Moreover, Spanish pronouns usually correspond in gender and number with their antecedent.

✎ REVIEW

Circle the pronouns in the sentences below.
- Draw an arrow from the pronoun to its antecedent, or antecedents if there is more than one.

1. Did Mary call Peter? Yes, she called him last night.

2. That coat and dress are elegant but they are expensive.

3. Isabel baked the cookies herself.

4. Robert and I are very tired. We went out last night.

5. The book is not on the desk. Where is it?

WHAT IS A SUBJECT PRONOUN?

A **SUBJECT PRONOUN** is a pronoun used
as a subject of a verb.

> *He* worked while *she* read.
> Who worked? ANSWER: He.
> *He* is the subject of the verb *worked*.
>
> Who read? ANSWER: She.
> *She* is the subject of the verb *read*.

Subject pronouns are divided into three groups: 1ˢᵗ, 2ⁿᵈ, and 3ʳᵈ person pronouns. The word **PERSON** in this instance does not necessarily mean a human being. It is a grammatical term that can refer to any noun.

IN ENGLISH

Here is a list of subject pronouns.

1ˢᵀ PERSON

I → the person speaking → SINGULAR
we → the person speaking plus others → PLURAL

> *Mary and I* are free this evening. *We* are going out.

2ⁿᵈ PERSON

you → the person or persons spoken to → SINGULAR or PLURAL

> *Paul*, do *you* sing folksongs?
> *Peter, Paul and Mary*, do *you* sing folksongs?

3ʳᵈ PERSON

he, she, it → the person or object spoken about → SINGULAR
they → the persons or objects spoken about → PLURAL

> *Mary and Paul* are free this evening. *They* are going out.

IN SPANISH

Spanish subject pronouns are also identified as 1ˢᵗ, 2ⁿᵈ and 3ʳᵈ persons. They are usually divided into singular and plural and presented in the following order.

SINGULAR

1ˢᵀ PERSON	I	yo
2ⁿᵈ PERSON	you	tú
3ʳᵈ PERSON	he	él
	she	ella
	you	usted

PLURAL

1ST PERSON	we	nosotros nosotras
2ND PERSON	you	vosotros vosotras
3RD PERSON	they	ellos ellas
	you	ustedes

As you can see above, there are three English subject pronouns that have more than one equivalent in Spanish: *you* (**tú, usted, vosotros, vosotras,** or **ustedes**), *we* (**nosotros** or **nosotras**), and *they* (**ellos** or **ellas**). Also there is one English subject pronoun, *it*, that has no equivalent in Spanish because it is generally not expressed.

Although *you* is a 2nd person pronoun since *you* is the person spoken to, two of its forms, **usted** and **ustedes**, are listed with 3rd person pronouns because they use the same forms as other 3rd person pronouns.

Let us look at the English subject pronouns that are either not expressed in Spanish *(it)*, or that have more than one Spanish equivalent *(you, we* and *they)*.

"YOU" (2nd PERSON SINGULAR AND PLURAL)

IN ENGLISH

The same pronoun "you" is used to address one or more than one person.

> Mary, are *you* coming with me?
> Mary and Paul, are *you* coming with me?

The same pronoun "you" is used to address the President of the United States or your dog.

> Do *you* have any questions, Mr. President?
> *You* are a good dog, Heidi.

IN SPANISH

There are several words for "you" in Spanish. **Tú, vosotros** and **vosotras** are called the FAMILIAR FORM or the FAMILIAR "YOU." **Usted** and **ustedes** are called the FORMAL FORM or the FORMAL "YOU."

FAMILIAR "YOU" → TÚ, VOSOTROS OR VOSOTRAS

The familiar forms of "you" are used to address members of one's family (notice that the word "familiar" is similar to the word "family"), persons you call by their first name, children, and pets.

1. to address one person → **tú** (2nd person singular)

> *Mary, how are you?*
> |
> **tú**

> *John, how are you?*
> |
> **tú**

2. to address more than one person → **vosotros** or **vosotras** (2nd person plural)

- to address a group of two or more males → **vosotros** 90

> *John and Paul, how are you?*
> └──┬──┘ |
> masc. pl.   **vosotros** (masc. pl.)

- to address a group of two or more females → **vosotras**

> *Mary and Gloria, how are you?*
> └──────┘ |
> fem. pl.   **vosotras** (fem. pl.)

- to address a group of males and females → **vosotros**

> *John, Gloria and Mary, how are you?*
> | | | |
> masc. fem.   fem.   **vosotros** (masc. pl.) 100

The familiar plural forms **vosotros** and **vosotras** are used only in Spain. In Latin America **ustedes** is used as the plural of **tú** (see below).

FORMAL "YOU" → USTED AND USTEDES

The formal forms of "you" are used to address persons you do not know well enough to call by a first name or to whom you should show respect (Ms. Smith, Mr. Jones, Dr. Anderson, Professor Gómez). 110

1. to address one person → **usted** (singular)

> *Mr. García, how are you?*
> |
> **usted**

> *Mrs. García, how are you?*
> |
> **usted**

2. to address a group of males or females → **ustedes** (plural)

> *Professor Gómez and Mrs. García, how are you?*
> | | |
> masc. sing.   fem. sing.   **ustedes** 120

In Latin America **ustedes** is the plural of both the familiar and formal forms.

CAREFUL — If in doubt as to whether to use the familiar or formal forms when addressing an adult, use the formal forms. They show respect for the person you are talking to and use of familiar forms might be considered rude.

CHOOSING THE PROPER FORM OF "YOU"

In order to choose the correct form of "you" in Spanish, you should go through the following steps:

1. Determine whether the familiar or formal form is appropriate.

2. If the familiar form is appropriate, determine how many persons are being addressed:
   A. one person → **tú**

   B. more than one person:

   ▪ IN LATIN AMERICA → **ustedes**

   ▪ IN SPAIN → determine the gender of the persons being addressed:
   a) a group of males or males and females → **vosotros**
   b) a group of females → **vosotras**

3. If the formal form is appropriate, determine how many persons are being addressed:
   A. one person → **usted**

   B. more than one person → **ustedes**

Here is a chart you can use as a reference.

		ENGLISH	SPANISH	
			SPAIN	LATIN AMERICA
FAMILIAR	SINGULAR	*you*	**tú**	**tú**
	PLURAL	*you*	**vosotros** **vosotras**	**ustedes**
FORMAL	SINGULAR	*you*	**usted**	**usted**
	PLURAL	*you*	**ustedes**	**ustedes**

Let's find the Spanish equivalent for *you* in the following sentences:

*John, are **you** coming with us?*
   FAMILIAR OR FORMAL: familiar
   SINGULAR OR PLURAL: singular *(John)*
   SELECTION: **tú**

Juan, ¿vienes **tú** con nosotros?

*Isabel and Gloria, are **you** coming with us?*
 FAMILIAR OR FORMAL: familiar
 SINGULAR OR PLURAL: plural *(Isabel, Gloria)*
 SPAIN OR LATIN AMERICA: Spain
 MALES, FEMALES OR MIXED GROUP: females
 SELECTION: **vosotras**

Isabel y Gloria, ¿venís **vosotras** con nosotros?

*Vincent and John, are **you** coming with us?*
 FAMILIAR OR FORMAL: familiar
 SINGULAR OR PLURAL: plural *(Vincent, John)*
 SPAIN OR LATIN AMERICA: Latin America
 SELECTION: **ustedes**

Vicente y Juan, ¿vienen **ustedes** con nosotros?

*Mr. President, are **you** coming with us?*
 FAMILIAR OR FORMAL: formal
 SINGULAR OR PLURAL: singular *(Mr. President)*
 SELECTION: **usted**

Señor Presidente, ¿viene **usted** con nosotros?

*Mr. and Mrs. Lado, are **you** coming with us?*
 FAMILIAR OR FORMAL: formal
 SINGULAR OR PLURAL: plural *(Mr., Mrs. Lado)*
 SELECTION: **ustedes**

Señor y señora Lado, ¿vienen **ustedes** con nosotros?

"IT" (3ᴿᴰ PERSON SINGULAR)

IN ENGLISH

Whenever you are speaking about one thing or idea, you use the subject pronoun "it."

> Where is the book? *It* is on the table.
> John has an idea. *It* is very interesting.

IN SPANISH

The subject pronoun *it* is not generally expressed.

> ¿Dónde está el libro? **Está** sobre la mesa.
> *It* is understood as part of the verb **está**.
> *Where is the book? **It is** on the table.*

"WE" (1ˢᵀ PERSON PLURAL)

IN ENGLISH

The subject pronoun "we" refers to the person speaking plus others.

> *John and I* are going to the movies.
> *We* are leaving at 7:00.

IN SPANISH

The subject pronoun used depends on the gender of the noun *we* replaces. In other words, the Spanish pronoun must agree with the gender of the antecedent.

- masculine antecedents → **nosotros**

    Juan y yo vamos al cine. **Nosotros** salimos a las 7.
    | | |
    masc. masc. (man speaking) masc. pl.
    antecedents   pronoun
    John and I are going to the movies. ***We** are leaving at 7:00.*

- feminine antecedent → **nosotras**

    María y yo vamos al cine. **Nosotras** salimos a las 7.
    | | |
    fem.   fem. (woman speaking)   fem. pl.
    antecedents   pronoun
    Mary and I are going to the movies. ***We** are leaving at 7:00.*

- antecedents of different genders → **nosotros**

    Juan, María y yo vamos al cine. **Nosotros** salimos a las 7.
    | | |
    masc. fem. masc. or fem.   masc. pl.
    └ antecedents ┘   pronoun
    John, Mary and I are going to the movies. ***We** are leaving at 7:00.*

"THEY" (3ᴿᴰ PERSON PLURAL)

IN ENGLISH

Whenever you are speaking about more than one person or object, you use the subject pronoun "they."

> My brothers play tennis. *They* practice a lot.
> My sisters play soccer. *They* practice every day.
> Where are the books? *They* are on the table.

IN SPANISH

The subject pronoun used depends on the gender of the noun *they* replaces. In other words, the Spanish pronoun must agree with the gender of the antecedent.

- masculine antecedent → **ellos**

    Mis hermanos juegan al tenis. **Ellos** practican cada día.
    |
    masc. pl.   masc. pl.
    antecedent   pronoun
    My brothers play tennis. ***They** practice every day.*

- feminine antecedent → **ellas**

    Mis hermanas juegan al fútbol. **Ellas** practican cada día.
    fem. pl.   fem. pl.
    antecedent   pronoun
    *My sisters play soccer. **They** practice every day.*

- antecedents of different genders → **ellos**

    Juan, María y Gloria juegan al fútbol. **Ellos** practican cada día.
    masc. fem.   fem.   masc. pl.
    └─ antecedents ─┘   pronoun
    *John, Mary and Gloria play soccer. **They** practice every day.*

Just as the subject pronoun *it* is not expressed in Spanish, the subject pronoun *they* is not expressed when *they* refers to something other than people.

    ¿Dónde están los libros? **Están** sobre la mesa.
    They is understood as part of the verb **están**.
    *Where are the books? **They are** on the table.*

✎ REVIEW

A. Write the corresponding person and number for the words in italics.
- Write the Spanish subject pronoun that you would use to replace the words in italics. If no pronoun is needed, write "0" in the space under Spanish subject pronoun.

	PERSON	NUMBER	SPANISH SUBJECT PRONOUN
1. *I* am very tired.	____	____	____
2. *It* is very hot outside.	____	____	____
3. *Mary and I* are leaving today.	____	____	____
4. *My keys* are here.	____	____	____
5. Where does *your son* live?	____	____	____
6. *Gloria and Anita* are friends.	____	____	____

B. Write the form of "you" that would be used in each instance.

	SPAIN	LATIN AMERICA
1. Mr. and Mrs. Fuentes, how are *you*?	_____	_____
2. Teresa, where are *you* going?	_____	_____

250

260

3. Señorita Acosta, will *you* please
   finish this report?   _____ _____

4. Come on children, *you* must
   go to bed.   _____ _____

5. Daddy, will *you* play a game
   with me?   _____ _____

6. Professor Suárez, *you* haven't given
   us our homework for tomorrow.   _____ _____

STUDY TIPS — SUBJECT PRONOUNS

Flashcards

Create a flashcard for each subject pronoun (1st, 2nd, and 3rd person singular and plural). You'll add the other forms of the pronoun when you
learn them (see *Study Tips — Object Pronouns and their Position*, p. 155).

yo	*I*
ella	*she*

Practice

You'll practice subject pronouns when you practice conjugating verbs
(see *Study Tips — Verb Conjugations*, p. 48).

WHAT IS A VERB CONJUGATION?

A **VERB CONJUGATION** is a list of the six possible forms of the
verb for a particular tense. For each tense, there is
one verb form for each of the six persons
used as the subject of the verb.

> I am
> you are
> he, she, it is
> we are
> you are
> they are

Different tenses have different verb forms, but the princi-
ple of conjugation remains the same. In this chapter all
our examples are in the present tense (see *What is the
Present Tense?*, p. 67).

IN ENGLISH

The verb *to be* conjugated above is the English verb that
changes the most; it has three forms: *am, are,* and *is.* (The
initial vowel is often replaced by an apostrophe: *I'm,
you're, he's.*) Other English verbs only have two forms such
as the verb *to sing.*

SINGULAR

1ST PERSON	I *sing*
2ND PERSON	you *sing*
3RD PERSON	he *sings* she *sings* it *sings*

PLURAL

1ST PERSON	we *sing*
2ND PERSON	you *sing*
3RD PERSON	they *sing*

Because English verbs change so little, it isn't necessary
to learn "to conjugate a verb;" that is, to list all its possible
forms. For most verbs, it is much simpler to say that the
verb adds an "-s" in the 3rd person singular.

IN SPANISH

Unlike English, Spanish verb forms change from one person to another so that when you learn a new verb, you

must also learn how to conjugate it. First, you must establish whether the verb is regular or irregular.

- Verbs whose forms follow a predictable pattern are called REGULAR VERBS. Only one example must be memorized and the pattern can then be applied to other verbs in the same group.

- Verbs whose forms do not follow a predictable pattern are called IRREGULAR VERBS. The conjugation of these verbs must be memorized individually.

CHOOSING THE PROPER "PERSON" (see p. 33)

Below is the conjugation of the regular verb **cantar** *(to sing)*. Notice that each of the six persons has its own ending and that different pronouns belonging to the same person have the same verb form. Since the subject pronouns **usted** and **ustedes** use the verb form of the 3ʳᵈ person, they are listed with that person. Therefore, **él, ella** and **usted**, have the same verb form: **canta**.

SINGULAR

1ˢᵗ PERSON	yo canto	*I sing*
2ᴺᴰ PERSON	tú cantas	*you sing*
3ᴿᴰ PERSON	él canta	*he sings, it sings*
	ella canta	*she sings, it sings*
	usted canta	*you sing*

PLURAL

1ˢᵗ PERSON	nosotros cantamos	*we sing*[1]
	nosotras cantamos	*we sing*
2ᴺᴰ PERSON	vosotros cantáis	*you sing*
	vosotras cantáis	*you sing*
3ᴿᴰ PERSON	ellos cantan	*they sing*
	ellas cantan	*they sing*
	ustedes cantan	*you sing*

To choose the proper verb form, it is important to identify the person (1ˢᵗ, 2ⁿᵈ or 3ʳᵈ) and the number (singular or plural) of the subject.

1ˢᵗ PERSON SINGULAR — The subject is always **yo** *(I)*.

Generalmente **yo canto** bien.
Generally I sing well.

Notice that **yo** is not capitalized except when it is the first word of a sentence.

[1]Many textbooks only list **nosotros** and **vosotros**. The same verb form applies to **nosotras** and **vosotras**.

2ᴺᴰ PERSON SINGULAR — The subject is always **tú** *(you).*

> Juan, **tú cantas** muy bien.
> *John, you sing very well.*

3ᴿᴰ PERSON SINGULAR — The subject can be expressed in one of four ways:

1. the 3ʳᵈ person singular masculine pronoun **él** *(he)* and the 3ʳᵈ person singular feminine pronoun **ella** *(she)*

> Generalmente **él canta** muy bien.
> *Generally he sings very well.*

> Generalmente **ella canta** muy bien.
> *Generally she sings very well.*

2. the singular pronoun **usted** *(you)*

> Señor Gómez, **usted canta** muy bien.
> *Mr. Gómez, you sing very well.*

> Señorita Gómez, **usted canta** muy bien.
> *Miss Gómez, you sing very well.*

The pronoun **usted** is generally abbreviated as **Ud.** The abbreviation is used far more frequently than the entire word.

3. a proper noun

> María **canta** muy bien.
> *Mary sings very well.*

> Pedro **canta** muy bien.
> *Peter sings very well.*

> El señor García **canta** muy bien.
> *Mr. Garcia sings very well.*

In these three sentences the proper noun could be replaced by the pronoun *she* (**ella** fem.) or *he* (**él** masc.) so that you must use the 3ʳᵈ person singular form of the verb.

4. a singular common noun

> El hombre **canta** muy bien.
> *The man sings very well.*

> La niña **canta** muy bien.
> *The girl sings very well.*

In these two sentences the common noun could be replaced by the pronoun *she* (**ella** fem.) or *he* (**él** masc.) so that you must use the 3ʳᵈ person singular form of the verb.

Remember that the subject pronoun *it* has no Spanish equivalent. It is generally not expressed but rather it is understood as part of the verb. (See *What is a Subject Pronoun?*, p. 33.)

Juan y María tienen un párajo. **Canta** muy bien.
John and Mary have a bird. It sings very well.

1ˢᵗ PERSON PLURAL — The subject can be expressed in one of two ways:

1. the 1ˢᵗ person plural pronoun **nosotros** or **nosotras** *(we)*

130

Nosotros **cantamos** bien.
We sing well.

2. a multiple subject in which the speaker is included

Miguel, Gloria y yo **cantamos** muy bien.

nosotros

Michael, Gloria and I sing very well.

The subjects *Michael, Gloria and I* could be replaced by the pronoun *we*, so that you must use the 1ˢᵗ person plural form of the verb.

140

2ᴺᴰ PERSON PLURAL — The subject can be expressed in one of two ways:

1. the 2ⁿᵈ person plural pronoun **vosotros** or **vosotras** *(you)*

Vosotras **cantáis** bien.
You sing well.

2. a multiple subject in which the speaker is not included

Juan y tú **cantáis** muy bien.
John and you sing very well.

In this sentence *John* (whom you would address with the **tú** form) and *you* (whom you also address with the **tú** form) could be replaced by the pronoun *you*, so that you must use the 2ⁿᵈ person plural form of the verb.

150

The familiar plural *you* form of the verb (the **vosotros** form) is used only in Spain when you are speaking to two or more persons with whom you would use **tú** individually. Many beginning Spanish textbooks do not emphasize or practice the **vosotros** form. Your instructor will inform you if you need to learn the **vosotros** forms of verbs or not.

3ᴺᴰ PERSON PLURAL — The subject can be expressed in one of four ways:

160

1. the 3ʳᵈ person plural masculine pronoun **ellos** *(they)* and the 3ʳᵈ person plural feminine pronoun **ellas** *(they)*

Ellos **cantan** muy bien.
They sing very well.

Ellas **cantan** muy bien.
They sing very well.

2. the plural pronoun **ustedes** *(you)*

> Elena y Francisco, **ustedes cantan** muy bien.
> *Helen and Francis, **you sing** very well.*

In this sentence Helen (whom you would address with the **tú** form) and Francis (whom you also address with the **tú** form) could be replaced by the **ustedes** form of *you,* so that you must use the 3rd person plural form of the verb.

170

The pronoun **ustedes** is generally abbreviated as **Uds.** The abbreviation is used far more frequently than the entire word.

3. two or more proper or common nouns

> Isabel, Gloria y Roberto cantan muy bien.
> fem. + fem. + masc. (ellos)
>
> *Isabel, Gloria and Robert sing very well.*
>
> La chica y su padre cantan muy bien.
> fem. + masc. (ellos)
>
> *The girl and her father sing very well.*

180

4. a plural noun

> Las chicas cantan muy bien.
> fem. pl. (ellas)
>
> *The girls sing very well.*

190

Just as the subject pronoun *it* has no Spanish equivalent, *they* has no Spanish equivalent when it does not refer to persons (see *What is a Subject Pronoun?*, p. 33).

> María tiene dos párajos. **Cantan** muy bien.
> *Mary has two birds. **They sing** very well.*

HOW TO CONJUGATE A VERB

A Spanish verb, whether regular or irregular, is composed of two parts:

1. The STEM, also called the "root," is the part of the verb left after dropping the last two letters from the infinitive (see *What is the Infinitive?*, p. 25).

200

INFINITIVE	STEM
cantar	cant-
comer	com-
vivir	viv-

In regular verbs the stem usually remains the same throughout a conjugation. However, in certain verbs called STEM-CHANGING VERBS, the stem will change in a minor way. (Your textbook will identify these verbs.)

2. The ENDING is the letter or letters added to the stem and which change for each person in the conjugation of regular and irregular verbs.

Regular verbs are divided into three GROUPS, also called CON-JUGATIONS, identified by the infinitive ending of the verb.

-ar	-er	-ir
1st group	2nd group	3rd group

Each of the three verb groups has its own set of endings for each tense (see *What is Meant by Tense?*, p. 64). Memorizing the conjugation of one sample verb for each group enables you to conjugate all the other regular verbs belonging to that group.

As an example of the steps to follow to conjugate a regular verb, let us look at verbs of the 1st group (-ar verbs), that is, verbs like **hablar** *(to speak)* and **tomar** *(to take)* that follow the pattern of **cantar** *(to sing)* conjugated on p. 42.

1. Identify the group of the verb by its infinitive ending.

    hablar
    tomar → -ar verbs or 1st conjugation or group

2. Find the verb stem by removing the infinitive ending.

    habl-
    tom-

3. Add the ending that agrees with the subject.

yo	hablo	yo	tomo
tú	hablas	tú	tomas
él / ella / usted	habla	él / ella / usted	toma
nosotros / nosotras	hablamos	nosotros / nosotras	tomamos
vosotros / vosotras	habláis	vosotros / vosotras	tomáis
ellos / ellas / ustedes	hablan	ellos / ellas / ustedes	toman

The endings of regular verbs belonging to the other groups are different, but the process of conjugation is the same. Just follow the three steps above.

As irregular verbs are introduced in your textbook, their entire conjugation will be given. Be sure to memorize them because many common verbs are irregular (**tener**, *to have*; **ser**, *to be*; **ir**, *to go*; **hacer**, *to make*, for example).

OMITTING THE SUBJECT PRONOUN IN SPANISH

As you can see the Spanish verb ending indicates the subject. For instance, **hablo** can only have **yo** *(I)* as a subject. When the verb ending can only refer to one subject, the subject pronoun is often omitted. 260

hablo	*I speak*
hablas	*you speak*
hablamos	*we speak*
habláis	*you speak*

However, since the verb ending of the 3rd person singular and plural forms can refer to several different persons, it is often necessary to include the pronoun. 270

habla could be	**él** habla	*he speaks*
	ella habla	*she speaks*
	Ud. habla	*you speak*
hablan could be	**ellos** hablan	*they speak*
	ellas hablan	*they speak*
	Uds. hablan	*you speak*

✎ REVIEW

Write the stem and conjugate the regular verb **comprar** *(to buy)*.

STEM: _____

yo _____	nosotros_____
tú _____	vosotros _____
él	ellos
ella _____	ellas _____
Ud.	Uds.

STUDY TIPS — VERB CONJUGATIONS (SEE P. 48)

Pattern (see *Tips for Learning Word Forms,* pp. 3-4)

1. Start by looking for a pattern within the conjugation of the verb itself. Let's look at similarities between the various conjugations of regular verbs: **preguntar** *(to ask)*, **aprender** *(to learn)*, **vivir** *(to live)*.

		preguntar	aprender	vivir
Infinitive:		preguntar	aprender	vivir
Stem:		pregunt-	aprend-	viv-
1ˢᵗ per. sing.	(yo)	pregunto	aprendo	vivo
2ⁿᵈ per. sing.	(tú)	preguntas	aprendes	vives
3ʳᵈ per. sing.	(él, etc.)	pregunta	aprende	vive
1ˢᵗ per. pl.	(nosotros)	preguntamos	aprendemos	vivimos
2ⁿᵈ per. pl.	(vosotros)	preguntáis	aprendéis	vivís
3ʳᵈ per. pl.	(ellos, etc.)	preguntan	aprenden	viven

What pattern do you see?
- 1ˢᵗ pers. sing.: all end in **-o**
- 2ⁿᵈ pers. sing.: all end in **-s**, **-ar** and **-er** verbs add the **-s** after the vowel of the infinitive (**-a** and **-e**), but **-ir** verbs add the **-s** after the vowel **-e**
- 3ʳᵈ pers. sing.: **-ar** and **-er** verbs end with the vowel of the infinitive (**-a** and **-e**), but **-ir** verbs end with the vowel **-e** (same vowel as used for 2ⁿᵈ pers. sing.)
- 1ˢᵗ pers. pl.: all end with **-mos** after the vowel of the infinitive (**-a, -e** and **-i**)
- 2ⁿᵈ pers. pl.: all end in **-is** after the vowel of the infinitive on which there is an accent (**-á, -é** and **-í**)
- 3ʳᵈ pers. pl.: all end in **-n**, **-ar** and **-er** verbs add the **-n** after the vowel of the infinitive (**-a** and **-e**), but **-ir** verbs add the **-n** after the vowel **-e** (same vowel as used for 2ⁿᵈ and 3ʳᵈ pers. sing.)

2. Whenever you learn a new verb, look for similarities in the pattern with another verb. Here are two stem-changing verb patterns.

cont**ar** *(to count)*

cuento	contamos
cuentas	contáis
cuenta	**cuentan**

pod**er** *(to be able to)*

puedo	podemos
puedes	podéis
puede	**pueden**

pens**ar** *(to think)*

pienso	pensamos
piensas	pensáis
piensa	**piensan**

entend**er** *(to understand)*

entiendo	entendemos
entiendes	entendéis
entiende	**entienden**

3. Even irregular verbs will have some type of pattern. For instance, make a list of the similarities between the conjugation of **dar** *(to give)*, **ir** *(to go)*, **ser** *(to be)*, **estar** *(to be)*.

Infinitive:		dar	ir	ser	estar
1ˢᵗ per. sing.	(yo)	doy	voy	soy	estoy
2ⁿᵈ per. sing.	(tú)	das	vas	eres	estás
3ʳᵈ per. sing.	(él, etc.)	da	va	es	está
1ˢᵗ per. pl.	(nosotros)	damos	vamos	somos	estamos
2ⁿᵈ per. pl.	(vosotros)	dais	vais	sois	estáis
3ʳᵈ per. pl.	(ellos, etc.)	dan	van	son	están

What similarities did you see? Compare your list to the one below.
- 1ˢᵗ pers. sing.: all end in **-oy** (instead of **-o** like regular verbs)
- 2ⁿᵈ pers. sing.: all end in **-s** like regular verbs

- 1ˢᵗ pers. pl.: all end in **–mos** like regular verbs
- 3ʳᵈ pers. pl.: all end in **–n** like regular verbs
- the forms of **ir** and **dar** are alike except for the first letter
- **ir** and **dar** are conjugated as if they were regular **–ar** verbs, except for the 1ˢᵗ pers. sing. and accents

3. As new verb conjugations are introduced, more and more similarities and patterns will become evident. Take the time to look for them; it will make learning conjugations much easier and faster.

Flashcards—See also *Study Tips – Tenses*, p. 66.

To review verbs and their conjugations, take out the flashcards you created to learn the meaning of the verbs (see p. 28) and add the following information on the Spanish side:

1. Indicate if the verb is regular (reg.) or irregular (irreg.) so that you can review irregular verbs separately.

> bailar *(reg.)*   to dance
> hacer *(irreg.)*   to do, to make

2. If the verb is irregular but shares a pattern with another verb, indicate the other verb.

> merecer *(irreg.)*   to deserve
> *(like* conocer = *to know)*

3. If the verb is irregular only in one form, write down that it is regular except for that one form.

> salir *(irreg.)*   to leave
> (regular -ir, except **yo salgo**)

4. If the verb is a stem-changing verb, indicate its type (**ie, ue, i**) in parentheses (see your textbook for types of stem-changing verbs).

> pensar (**ie**)   to think
> volver (**ue**)   to return
> pedir (**i**)   to ask for, to request

Practice

1. As you learn the different forms of a verb, write them down as many times as you need to so that you are able to write them without using your textbook.
2. Practice using the various forms out of order, so that if you are asked a question you can respond without going through the entire conjugation in your head.
3. Apply the pattern you've just learned to another verb with the same conjugation, if there is one.
4. Be sure to do the exercises that follow the introduction of a new conjugation in your textbook and workbook. If you have to refer to your textbook, notes or cards to do the exercises, you haven't really learned the forms.
5. Create and write down your own sentences using the different forms of the verb, or preferably with other verbs that are conjugated the same way.

CHAPTER

WHAT ARE AUXILIARY VERBS?

¹
A verb is called an AUXILIARY VERB or HELPING VERB when
it helps another verb, called the MAIN VERB,
form one of its tenses.

He *has been gone* two weeks.	*has*	AUXILIARY VERB
	been	AUXILIARY VERB
	gone	MAIN VERB

IN ENGLISH

There are three auxiliary verbs, *to have, to be*, and *to do*,
as well as a series of auxiliary words such as *will, would,*
may, must, can, could that are used to change the tense
and meaning of the main verb.

- Auxiliaries are used primarily to indicate the tense of
  the main verb (present, past, future — see *What is Meant*
  by Tense?, p.64).

  Mary *is reading* a book.   PRESENT
  |
  auxiliary *to be*

  Mary *has read* a book.   PAST
  |
  auxiliary *to have*

  Mary *will read* a book.   FUTURE
  |
  auxiliary *will*

- The auxiliary verb *to do* is used to help formulate questions and to make sentences negative (see *What are*
  Declarative and Interrogative Sentences?, p. 56 and *What*
  are Affirmative and Negative Sentences?, p. 53).

  Does Mary *read* a book?   INTERROGATIVE SENTENCE
  Mary *does* not *read* a book.   NEGATIVE SENTENCE

IN SPANISH

There are three verbs that can be used as auxiliary verbs:
estar *(to be)*, **haber** *(to have)*, and **ser** *(to be)*. The other
English auxiliaries such as *do, does, did, will*, or *would* do
not exist as auxiliaries in Spanish. Their meaning is con-
veyed either by a different structure or by the form of the
main verb. You will find more on this topic under the
chapters dealing with the different tenses.

A verb tense composed of an auxiliary verb plus a main verb is called a COMPOUND TENSE, as opposed to a SIMPLE TENSE which is a tense composed of only the main verb.

> Julia **estudia**.
> simple tense
> present tense of **estudiar**
> *Julia studies.*

> Julia **ha estudiado**.
> auxiliary main
> verb   verb
> compound tense
> present perfect tense of **estudiar**
> *Julia has studied.*

Auxiliary verbs used to indicate tense and voice

The auxiliary verbs **estar**, **haber**, and **ser** conjugated in the different tenses are followed by the participle of the main verb (see *What is a Participle?*, p. 73) to form three types of compound tenses in Spanish.

Let us look at examples of some compound tenses.

PERFECT TENSES — The auxiliary verb **haber** *(to have)* followed by the past participle of the main verb is used to form the many perfect tenses (see *What is a Participle?*, p. 73 and *What are the Perfect Tenses?*, p. 91).

- present perfect tense → present tense of **haber** + past participle of main verb

> Los estudiantes **han llegado**.
> auxiliary main
> verb   verb
> **haber**   **llegar** *(to arrive)*
> *The students have arrived.*

- past perfect tense → imperfect tense of **haber** + past participle of main verb

> Los estudiantes ya **habían llegado**.
> auxiliary   main
> verb   verb
> **haber**   **llegar** *(to arrive)*
> *The students had already arrived.*

You will learn other perfect tenses as your study of Spanish progresses.

80

PROGRESSIVE TENSES — The auxiliary verb **estar** *(to be)* followed by the present participle of the main verb is used to form the progressive tenses (see *What is a Participle?*, p. 73 and *What are the Progressive Tenses?*, p. 76).

- present progressive tense → present tense of **estar** + present participle of main verb

   Estoy leyendo un libro ahora.
   auxiliary main
   verb   verb
   estar   **leer** *(to read)*
   I am reading a book now.

90

- imperfect progressive tense → imperfect tense of **estar** + present participle of main verb

   Estábamos escuchando la radio.
   auxiliary   main
   verb   verb
   estar   escuchar *(to listen)*
   We were listening to the radio.

You will learn other progressive tenses as your study of Spanish progresses.

100

PASSIVE VOICE — The auxiliary verb **ser** *(to be)* is used to form the true passive voice (see *What is Meant by Active and Passive Voice?*, p. 104).

   El puente **fue construido** por los romanos.
   auxiliary main verb
   ser   construir *(to build)*
   *The bridge **was constructed** by the Romans.*

 REVIEW

Circle the auxiliary verbs in the following sentences.
- Cross out the English auxiliaries that are not used as auxiliaries in Spanish.

1. We will go to Argentina this year.

2. What are you doing?

3. Did you write your parents this week?

4. Tom had already graduated from high school by age sixteen.

5. Do you want to go to the movies with us?

WHAT ARE AFFIRMATIVE AND NEGATIVE SENTENCES?

A sentence can be classified according [1]
to whether or not the verb is negated,
that is, made negative with the word *not* or
another negative word such as *never, nobody*, or *nothing*.

An **AFFIRMATIVE SENTENCE** is a sentence whose verb is not negated. It states a fact that is.

> Spain is a country in Europe.
> John will work in the university.
> They liked to travel.

A **NEGATIVE SENTENCE** is a sentence whose verb is negated [10] with a negative word such as *no, not, never*. It states that a fact or situation is not true; it denies or negates the information it contains.

> Spain is *not* a country in Latin America.
> John will *not* work in a factory.
> They *never* liked to travel.

IN ENGLISH

An affirmative sentence can be changed to a negative sentence in one of two ways: [20]

1. by adding ***not*** after auxiliary words or auxiliary verbs (see *What are Auxiliary Verbs?*, p. 50)

AFFIRMATIVE	**NEGATIVE**
John *is* a student.	John is *not* a student.
Mary *can* do it.	Mary can*not* do it.
They *will* travel.	They will *not* travel.

   Frequently, the word *not* is attached to the verb and the letter "o" is replaced by an apostrophe; this is called a **CONTRACTION**: *is not → isn't; cannot → can't; will not → won't.* [30]

2. by adding the auxiliary verb ***do, does***, or ***did + not +*** the dictionary form of the main verb (*do* or *does* is used for negatives in the present tense and *did* for negatives in the past tense—see *What is the Present Tense?*, p. 67 and *What is the Past Tense?*, p. 69)

AFFIRMATIVE	NEGATIVE
We *study* a lot.	We *do not* study a lot.
Julia *writes* well.	Julia *does not* write well.
The plane *arrived*.	The plane *did not* arrive.

Frequently, *do, does,* or *did* is contracted with *not: do not* → *don't; does not* → *doesn't; did not* → *didn't.*

IN SPANISH

The basic rule for turning an affirmative sentence into a negative sentence is far simpler than in English. You merely place **no** in front of the conjugated verb.

AFFIRMATIVE	NEGATIVE
Estudiamos mucho.	No estudiamos mucho.
	| conjugated verb
*We **study** a lot.*	*We **do not** study a lot.*
Julia **escribe** bien.	Julia **no** escribe bien.
	| conjugated verb
*Julia **writes** well.*	*Julia **does not** write well.*
El avión **llegó**.	El avión **no** llegó.
	| conjugated verb
*The plane **arrived**.*	*The plane **didn't** arrive.*

CAREFUL — Remember that there is no equivalent for the auxiliary words *do, does, did* in Spanish; do not try to include them in negative sentences.

NEGATIVE WORDS

In both English and Spanish there are negative words that can be added to an affirmative sentence.

IN ENGLISH

The most common negative words are: *nothing, nobody, no one, never.*

I have *nothing* for you.
He *never* arrives on time.
When John is angry, he speaks to *no one (nobody).*

IN SPANISH

The most common negative words are **nada** (*nothing*), **nadie** (*nobody, no one*), and **nunca** (*never*). Often the negative word is used with **no** in the same sentence.

No tengo **nada** para ti.   80
*I have **nothing** for you. (I don't have **anything** for you.)*

Nunca llega a tiempo.
*He **never** arrives on time.*

Cuando Juan está enojado, **no** le habla a **nadie**.
*When John is angry, he speaks to **no one (nobody)**.*

The position of the negative word can change according
to its function in the sentence. (See *What are Indefinites and
Negatives?*, p. 195.)

NEGATIVE ANSWERS   90
IN ENGLISH

When answering a question negatively in English, both
no and *not* will often appear in the answer.

Do you live near the park? *No*, I do *not* live near the park.

IN SPANISH

Since both *no* and *not* have the Spanish equivalent **no**, the
word **no** will appear twice in the negative answer to the
above question in Spanish.

¿Vives cerca del parque? **No, no** vivo cerca del parque.   100
                          | |
                          no not
*Do you live near the park? No, I do **not** live near the park.*

✎ REVIEW

Write the negative of each sentence.
- Circle the words that indicate the negative in the sentences
  you have just written.
- Place an "x" over the words that would not appear in the
  Spanish negative sentence.

1. We want to leave class early.

   _____

2. He did his homework yesterday.

   _____

3. Teresa will go to Chile this summer.

   _____

4. Robert can go to the restaurant with us.

   _____

CHAPTER

WHAT ARE DECLARATIVE AND INTERROGATIVE SENTENCES?

A sentence can be classified as to whether it is making a statement or asking a question.

A **DECLARATIVE SENTENCE** is a sentence that makes a statement.

Columbus discovered America in 1492.

An **INTERROGATIVE SENTENCE** is a sentence that asks a question.

Did Columbus discover America in 1492?

In written language, an interrogative sentence always ends with a question mark.

IN ENGLISH

A declarative sentence can be changed to an interrogative sentence in one of two ways:

1. by adding the auxiliary verb *do, does,* or *did* before the subject and changing the main verb to the dictionary form of the verb (*do* and *does* are used to introduce a question in the present tense and *did* to introduce a question in the past tense — see *What is the Present Tense?*, p. 67 and *What is the Past Tense?*, p. 69)

DECLARATIVE SENTENCE	**INTERROGATIVE SENTENCE**
Philip *likes* sports cars.	*Does* Philip *like* sports cars?
present 3rd pers. sing.	present 3rd pers. sing. + dictionary form
Paul and Mary *sing* well.	*Do* Paul and Mary *sing* well?
present 3rd pers. pl.	present 3rd pers. pl. + dictionary form
Mark *went* to Mexico.	*Did* Mark *go* to Mexico?
past	past + dictionary form

2. by inverting the normal word order of subject + verb to verb + subject. This **INVERSION** process can only be used with auxiliary verbs (AV) or auxiliary words (AW). See *What are Auxiliary Verbs?*, p. 50.

DECLARATIVE SENTENCE	INTERROGATIVE SENTENCE
Paul is home.	*Is Paul* home?
subject + verb *to be*	verb *to be* + subject
You have received a letter.	*Have you received* a letter?
subject + AV + main verb	AV + subject + main verb
She will come tomorrow.	*Will she come* tomorrow?
subject + AW + main verb	AW + subject + main verb

IN SPANISH

Λ declarative sentence can be changed to an interrogative sentence by using the inversion process.

In a simple declarative sentence that consists of a subject + verb, the word order of the question is verb + subject.

DECLARATIVE SENTENCE	INTERROGATIVE SENTENCE
Juan estudia.	¿Estudia Juan?
subject verb	verb subject
John studies.	*Does John study?*
Los niños cantan.	¿Cantan los niños?
subject verb	verb subject
The children sing.	*Do the children sing?*

Notice that in written Spanish the question is signaled at both the beginning and end of the sentence. The punctuation mark at the beginning of the sentence looks like an upside-down question mark (¿); a question mark like the one in English is located at the end of the sentence (?).

TAG QUESTIONS

In both English and Spanish when you expect a yes-or-no answer, you can also transform a statement into a question by adding a short phrase at the end of the statement. This short phrase is called a TAG or TAG QUESTION.

IN ENGLISH

There are different tags, depending on the tense of the verb of the statement and whether the statement is affirmative or negative. For instance, affirmative statements take negative tags and negative statements take affirmative tags.

John and Mary *are* friends, *aren't they?*

affirmative statement   negative tag

John and Mary *aren't* friends, *are they?*

negative statement   affirmative tag

IN SPANISH

The words ¿**no?**, ¿**verdad?**, or ¿**no es verdad?** can be added to the end of an affirmative statement to form a tag question.

Juan y María son amigos, ¿**no?**
*John and Mary are friends, **aren't they?***

Trabajas mucho, ¿**verdad?**
*You work hard, **don't you?***

Hoy es miércoles, ¿**no es verdad?**
*Today is Wednesday, **isn't it?***

The word ¿**verdad?** is generally added to the end of a negative statement to form a tag question.

Juan y María no son amigos, ¿**verdad?**
*John and Mary aren't friends, **are they?***

 REVIEW

A. Using the inversion process, write the interrogative form of each declarative sentence on the line provided.
  ■ In the interrogative sentence, circle the English words that indicate the interrogative.
  ■ In the interrogative sentence, put an "x" over the words that would not appear in the Spanish question.

1. Richard and Kathy studied all evening.

_____

2. Your brother eats a lot.

_____

3. The girl's parents speak Spanish.

_____

B. Change the sentence to an interrogative sentence using a tag.

My mother and father went to the movies.

_____

WHAT ARE SOME EQUIVALENTS
OF "TO BE"?

IN ENGLISH

The verb *to be* has the following forms in the present tense: *I am; you are; he, she, it is; we are; you are; they are.* It is used in a variety of ways:

- to tell time

    It *is* 4:00.

- to discuss health

    John *isn't* very well.

- to describe traits and characteristics

    Mary *is* tall and blond.

- to tell ages

    I *am* twenty years old.

- to explain what there is or there are in specific places

    There *are* twenty-five students in the class.

IN SPANISH

There are various verbs used to express the English verb *to be:*

ENGLISH	SPANISH
	1. **ser** *(to be)*
to be	2. **estar** *(to be)*
	3. **tener** *(to have)*
there is, there are	4. **hay** (a form of *to have*)

Depending on what you want to say, you will have to use one of these four verbs. Here are a few rules to help you select the correct one:

1. TO BE = "SER"

Use a form of the verb **ser** when you are speaking about the following:

- to tell time

    It is 4:00.
    Son las cuatro.

1

10

20

30

- to show possession

> *That car is John's.*
> Ese coche es de Juan.

> *This book is yours.*
> Este libro es tuyo.

- to express nationality and origin

> *Mary is Spanish; she is from Madrid.*
> María es española; es de Madrid.

- with nouns to identify someone or something

> *Mr. Robles is a lawyer.*
> El señor Robles es abogado.

> *That building is the language laboratory.*
> Ese edificio es el laboratorio de lenguas.

- with adjectives to describe traits or characteristics

> *Mary is tall and blond.*
> María es alta y rubia.

2. To be = "Estar"

Use a form of the verb **estar** when you are speaking about the following:

- to express location

> *John and I are in the library.*
> Juan y yo estamos en la biblioteca.

> *The books are on the table.*
> Los libros están sobre la mesa.

- to discuss health

> *How are you?*
> ¿Cómo está Ud.?

> *Mary is fine but John is sick.*
> María está bien pero Juan está enfermo.

- with adjectives that describe a condition

> *I am tired and worried.*
> | |
>   adjectives of condition
> **Estoy** cansada y preocupada.

"Ser" vs. "estar"

As you can see above, when the verb *to be* is followed by an adjective, both **ser** and **estar** can be used. You will need to decide what type of adjective is used in order to select the appropriate verb.

- with adjectives that describe physical characteristics and personality traits → **ser**

80

> *My house is modern.*
> |
>   characteristic
>
> Mi casa **es** moderna.

> > **Ser** is used because the adjective *modern* distinguishes the house from others. It answers the question: Which house is yours? or What is your house like?

> *Mary is nice.*
> |
>   trait
>
> María **es** simpática.

90

> > **Ser** is used because the adjective *nice* distinguishes Mary from other persons. It answers the question: What kind of person is Mary?

- adjectives that describe a condition → **estar**

> *My house is dirty.*
> |
>   condition
>
> Mi casa **está** sucia.

> > **Estar** is used because *dirty* describes a condition, not a characteristic of the house. It answers the question: What condition is the house in?

100

> *Mary is tired.*
> |
>   condition
>
> María **está** cansada.

> > **Estar** is used because the adjective *tired* describes a condition, not a characteristic of Mary. It answers the question: What is Mary's condition?

In a question, a different type of information is being requested depending on whether **ser** or **estar** is used.

110

> ¿Cómo **es** María?

> > Use of **ser** → What is Mary like? What are her traits?

> ¿Cómo **está** María?

> > Use of **estar** → How is Mary? What is her condition? How is she feeling?

3. TO BE = "TENER" (to have)

Sometimes the English expression *to be* + adjective is expressed with the Spanish verb *to have* (**tener**) + noun. These idiomatic expressions using **tener** + noun must be memorized.

120

Here are a few examples:

I am hungry.
    | |
to be + adjective
Tengo hambre.
    | |
to have + noun [word-for-word: I *have* hunger]

I am twenty years old.
  | |
to be + adjective
Tengo veinte años.
    | |
to have + noun [word-for-word: I *have* twenty years]

130

4. THERE IS, THERE ARE = "HAY"

The English expressions *there is* or *there are* are translated with the Spanish word **hay**. **Hay** is INVARIABLE; that is, it does not change form since it can be either singular or plural.

There is a book on the table.
          |
    singular noun
Hay un libro sobre la mesa.

140

There are many books on the table.
               |
      plural noun
Hay muchos libros sobre la mesa.

You must learn to use this common expression correctly and not confuse it with **estar**. To avoid using the wrong verb, see if you can replace the "is" or "are" of the English sentence with "there is" or "there are." If you can, you must use **hay**; if you can't, then **está** or **están** must be used.

150

On the table is a book.
            |
    there is [you can say: On the table *there is* a book.]
    |
    hay (to show presence)

The book is on the table.
        |
    is [you can't say: the book *there is* on the table]
    |
    está (to show location)

In the classroom are students.
               |
    there are [you can say: In the classroom *there are* students.]
    |

160

    hay (to show presence)

*The chairs and tables **are** in the classroom.*

are [you can't say: the chairs and the table *there are* in the
       classroom]
están (to show location)

✎ REVIEW

A. Decide if the italicized words are adjectives that describe a characteristic (CH) or a condition (C0).

 ■ Circle the infinitive form of the verb you would use in Spanish, **ser** or **estar**.

1. My car is *gray*.	CH	C0	**ser estar**
2. My car is *clean*.	CH	C0	**ser estar**
3. The students are *worried*.	CH	C0	**ser estar**
4. John is *tall, dark, and handsome*.	CH	C0	**ser estar**
5. I am *bored*.	CH	C0	**ser estar**
6. John, are you *sick?*	CH	C0	**ser estar**
7. Mary and I are *blond*.	CH	C0	**ser estar**

B. Decide if the words *is* or *are* express location (L) or express the presence (P) of people or things.

 ■ Circle the correct Spanish equivalent of *is* or *are*: **estar** or **hay**.

1. Our cars *are* in the garage.	L	P	**estar hay**
2. In the garage *are* several bicycles.	L	P	**estar hay**
3. Your lunch *is* on the table.	L	P	**estar hay**
4. For your lunch there *is* some soup.	L	P	**estar hay**

CHAPTER

17

WHAT IS MEANT BY TENSE?

1   The **TENSE** of a verb indicates when the action of the verb
takes place: at the present time, in the past, or in the
future. The word *tense* comes from the same word
as the Spanish word "tiempo," which means *time*.

I am studying PRESENT
I studied   PAST
I will study   FUTURE

As you can see in the above examples, just by putting
the verb in a different tense and without giving any addi-
10   tional information (such as "I am studying *now*," "I studied *yesterday*," "I will study *tomorrow*"), you can indicate
when the action of the verb takes place.

Tenses may be classified according to the way they are
formed. A **SIMPLE TENSE** consists of only one verb form (I *studied*), while a **COMPOUND TENSE** consists of one or more auxiliaries plus the main verb (I *am studying*, I *had been studying*).

In this section we will only consider tenses of the
indicative mood (see *What is Meant by Mood?*, p. 79).

IN ENGLISH

20   Listed below are the main tenses of the indicative mood
whose equivalents you will encounter in Spanish:

PRESENT

I study	PRESENT
I do study	PRESENT EMPHATIC
I am studying	PRESENT PROGRESSIVE

PAST

I studied	SIMPLE PAST
I did study	PAST EMPHATIC
I have studied	PRESENT PERFECT
30	I was studying	PAST PROGRESSIVE
I had studied	PAST PERFECT

FUTURE

I will study	FUTURE
I will have studied	FUTURE PERFECT

CONDITIONAL

I would study	CONDITIONAL
I would have studied	CONDITIONAL PERFECT

As you can see, there are only two simple tenses (present and simple past). All of the other tenses are compound tenses.

IN SPANISH

Listed below are the main tenses of the indicative mood that you will encounter in Spanish.

PRESENT

estudio	*I study, I do study*	PRESENT
	I am studying	
estoy estudiando	*I am studying*	PRESENT PROGRESSIVE

PAST

estudié	*I studied, I did study*	PRETERITE
estudiaba	*I used to study*	IMPERFECT
	I was studying	
estaba estudiando	*I was studying*	PAST PROGRESSIVE
he estudiado	*I have studied*	PRESENT PERFECT
había estudiado	*I had studied*	PAST PERFECT

FUTURE

estudiaré	*I will study*	FUTURE
habré estudiado	*I will have studied*	FUTURE PERFECT

CONDITIONAL[1]

estudiaría	*I would study*	CONDITIONAL
habría estudiado	*I would have studied*	CONDITIONAL PERFECT

As you can see, there are more simple tenses than in English (present, preterite, imperfect, future, and conditional). The compound tenses in Spanish are formed with the auxiliary verbs **estar** *(to be)* or **haber** *(to have)* + the main verb.

This handbook discusses the various tenses and their usage in separate chapters: *What is the Present Tense?*, p. 67; *What is the Past Tense?*, p. 69; *What is the Future Tense?*, p. 95; *What is the Conditional?*, p. 99; *What are the Progressive Tenses?*, p. 76; *What are the Perfect Tenses?*, p. 91. Verb tenses can be grouped according to the mood in which they are used (see *What is Meant by Mood?*, p. 79).

CAREFUL — Do not assume that tenses with the same name are used in the same way in English and in Spanish.

---

[1]The conditional tenses have been included because they have parallels in English. The subjunctive tenses have been omitted because they have no parallels in English.

Pattern (see *Tips for Learning Word Forms,* pp. 3-4)

Start by comparing the forms of the new tense to the other forms of that verb you already know, particularly the forms that are close in spelling and/or pronunciation. For example, as you learn the preterite tense of regular -**ar** verbs like **comprar** *(to buy)*, compare the forms to the present tense which you have already learned.

1. Identify the similarities with the other tenses. This will help you remember the new tense.

PRESENT:	PRETERITE:
compro	**compré**
compras	**compraste**
compra	**compró**
compramos	**compramos**
compráis	**comprasteis**
compran	**compraron**

- Stem is the same in the present and the preterite.
- 1st per. pl. is the same form in the present and preterite.

2. Identify the differences with the other tenses. This will help you avoid mixing them up.
   - The preterite tense has accent marks on the 1st and 3rd pers. sing. endings: compré, compró.
   - An accent mark sometimes distinguishes the present tense from the preterite.

compro	1st pers. sing. present
compró	3rd pers. sing. preterite

Flashcards

1. As you learn new tenses, separate the verb flashcards from your other cards and on the Spanish side note any irregular forms in that tense. If a verb has only one form that is irregular in a tense, make sure that you indicate that the other forms are regular.

INFINITIVE: poner	*to put*
PRESENT: pongo (all other forms regular)	*I put*
PRETERITE STEM: pus-; no accent on 1st & 2nd per. sing. (puse, puso)	
STEM FUTURE/CONDITIONAL: pondr-	

2. You will be able to recognize more patterns as you learn more verbs and tenses.

Practice

1. For simple tenses, see *Study Tips – Verb Conjugations,* p. 48.
2. For compound tenses, see *Study Tips – Perfect Tenses,* p. 94.
3. Apply the pattern you've just learned by writing and saying out loud another verb that follows the same pattern. For example, if you have learned that the irregular future stem of **poner** *(to put, place)* follows the "-**d** pattern," you can practice with other verbs with the same irregular future stem.

INFINITIVE	FUTURE STEM
poner	pondr-
tener (to have)	tendr-

4. Rewrite the practice sentences of a tense you've learned earlier using the new tense.

WHAT IS THE PRESENT TENSE?

The **PRESENT TENSE** indicates that the action is happening
at the present time. It can be at the moment the speaker
is speaking, a habitual action, or a general truth. 1

> I *see* you.
> He *smokes* constantly.
> The sun *rises* every day.

IN ENGLISH

There are three forms of the verb that indicate the present
tense. Each form has a slightly different meaning:

> Mary *studies* in the library.   PRESENT   10
> Mary *is studying* in the library.   PRESENT PROGRESSIVE
> Mary *does study* in the library.   PRESENT EMPHATIC

Depending on the information requested in a question,
you will automatically choose one of the three forms
above in your answer.

> Where does Mary study? She *studies* in the library.
> Where is Mary now? She *is studying* in the library.
> Does Mary study in the library? Yes, she *does [study* in the
> library]. 20

IN SPANISH

The present tense in Spanish is a simple tense formed by
adding a set of endings to the stem of the verb (see *What is
a Verb Conjugation?*, p. 41). Your textbook will give you the
present tense endings.

Unlike English, there is only one verb form to indicate
the present tense. The Spanish present tense is used to
express the meaning of the English present, present progressive, and present emphatic tenses.

> *Mary **studies** in the library.* 30
> estudia
>
> *Mary **is studying** in the library.*
> estudia
>
> *Mary **does study** in the library.*
> estudia

40

CAREFUL — Since the present is always indicated by the ending of the verb without an auxiliary verb such as *is* and *does*, you must not translate these English auxiliary verbs into Spanish. Simply put the main verb in the present tense.

✎ REVIEW

Fill in the proper form of the verb *to read* in the following answers.
- Write the Spanish verb form for sentences 2, 3 and 4.

1. What does Mary do all day?

   She _____.

   SPANISH VERB: **lee.**

2. What is Mary doing now?

   She _____.

   SPANISH VERB: _____

3. Does Mary read Spanish?

   Yes, she _____ Spanish.

   SPANISH VERB: _____

4. Has she read *Don Quixote?*

   No, but, she_____ it right now.

   SPANISH VERB: _____

WHAT IS THE PAST TENSE?

The **PAST TENSE** is used to express an action   1
that occurred in the past.

I *saw* you yesterday.

IN ENGLISH

There are several verb forms which indicate that the
action took place in the past.

I worked	SIMPLE PAST
I was working	PAST PROGRESSIVE
I used to work	WITH HELPING VERB USED TO
I did work	PAST EMPHATIC
I have worked	PRESENT PERFECT
I had worked	PAST PERFECT

The simple past is a simple tense; that is, it consists of one
word (*worked* in the example above). The other past tenses
are compound tenses; that is, they consist of more than
one word—an auxiliary plus a main verb *(was working, did
work)*. The present and past perfect tenses are discussed in
a separate section (see *What are the Perfect Tenses?*, p. 91).

IN SPANISH   20

As in English, there are several verb tenses that indicate
that an action took place in the past. Each tense has its
own set of endings and its own rules that tell us when
and how to use it. We are concerned here with only two
of the past tenses in Spanish: the preterite (**el pretérito**)
and the imperfect (**el imperfecto**).

THE PRETERITE

The preterite is a simple tense formed by adding a set of
endings to the stem of the verb. There are many irregular
verbs in the preterite tense. It is very important to learn   30
the preterite forms given in your textbook since the stems
of the preterite are also used as the base for other verb
forms.

The preterite generally translates as the simple past in
English.

hablé	*I spoke*
estudié	*I studied*

THE IMPERFECT

The imperfect is also a simple tense formed by adding a set of endings to the stem of the verb. The conjugation is very regular (there are only three irregular verbs in the imperfect tense).

There are two English verb forms that indicate that the imperfect should be used in Spanish.

1. the English verb form includes, or could include, *used to*

> *When I was little, **I played** in the park.*
>
> could be replaced by *used to play*
>
> Cuando yo era joven, **jugaba** en el parque.
>
> imperfect

2. the English verb form is in the past progressive tense, as in *was playing, were studying*

> ***I was studying** in my room.*
> **Yo estudiaba** en mi cuarto.
>
> imperfect

Except for these two verb forms, the English verb will not indicate to you whether you should use the imperfect or the preterite.

SELECTION OF THE PRETERITE OR IMPERFECT

When discussing and describing past events and activities, both the imperfect and the preterite are used. Whether to put a verb in the preterite or the imperfect often depends upon the context. As a general guideline, the difference in the two tenses is as follows:

> PRETERITE $\rightarrow$ tells "what happened" during a fixed period of time
>
> IMPERFECT $\rightarrow$ tells "how things used to be" or "what was going on" during a period of time

Here is an example. The same form of the verb *to go,* namely "went," is used in the two answers below: "I *went* to the park." However, the tense of the Spanish verb **ir** *(to go)* changes depending on the question asked.

- "What happened?"

> QUESTION: *What **did** you **do** yesterday?*
> ANSWER: *I **went** to the park.*
>
> The question and answer tell "what happened yesterday;" therefore, the Spanish equivalent of *did do* and *went* are in the preterite.

QUESTION: ¿Qué **hiciste** ayer?
ANSWER: **Fui** al parque.

- "How things used to be"

QUESTION: *What **did** you **do** when you were a child?*
ANSWER: *I **went** to the park.*
> The question and answer tell "how things used to be;" therefore, the Spanish equivalent of *did do* and *went* are in the imperfect.

QUESTION: ¿Qué **hacías** cuando eras joven?
ANSWER: **Iba** al parque.

90

- "What was going on?"

The imperfect and the preterite indicate actions that took place during the same time period in the past. You will often find the two tenses intermingled in a sentence or a story.

*I **was reading** when he **arrived**.*
> Both actions *reading* and *arrived* took place at the same time. What was going on? *I was reading* → imperfect. What happened? *He arrived* → preterite.

Leía cuando **llegó**.
   | |
imperfect   preterite

100

Consult your Spanish textbook for additional guidelines to help you choose the appropriate tense.

✎ REVIEW

Circle the verbs that would be put in the imperfect and underline the verbs that would be put in the preterite in Spanish.

Last summer, I *went* to Mexico with my family. Everyone *was* very excited when we *arrived* at the airport. While my mother *was checking* the luggage and my father *was handling* the tickets, my little sister Mary *ran* away. My parents *dropped* everything and *tried* to catch her, but she *ducked* behind the counter. Finally, a manager *grabbed* her and *brought* her back to us. She *was crying* because she *was* sad that she *was leaving* her dog Heidi for two weeks. Everyone *comforted* her and, finally, she *smiled* and *boarded* the plane.

Patterns (see *Tips for Learning Word Forms,* pp. 3-4 and *Study Tips – Verb Conjugations,* p. 48)

1. Regular verbs

STEM: infinitive minus -**ar**, -**er**, or -**ir**

ENDINGS: all have an accent on 1ˢᵗ and 3ʳᵈ pers. sing.

INFINITIVE: comprar *(to buy)*	volver *(to return)*	escribir *(to write)*
STEM: compr-	volv-	escrib-
compré compramos	volví volvimos	escribí escribimos
compraste comprasteis	volviste volvisteis	escribiste escribisteis
compró compraron	volvió volvieron	escribió escribieron

What similarities do you see? Here are some:

- 1ˢᵗ pers. sing.: -**ar** verbs end in -**é**; -**er** and -**ir** verbs end in -**í**
- 2ⁿᵈ pers. sing.: the endings of -**ar** and -**ir** verbs keep the vowel of the infinitive (-**a** and -**i**); the ending of -**er** verbs changes to -**i**
- 3ʳᵈ pers. sing.: all end in -**ó**; -**er** and -**ir** verbs add an -**i** before the -**ó**
- 1ˢᵗ pers. pl.: all end in -**mos**, the same as 1ˢᵗ pers. pl. of present tense
- 2ⁿᵈ pers. pl.: all end in -**steis**; the vowel preceding the -**steis** is the same as for 2ⁿᵈ pers. sing.
- 3ʳᵈ pers. pl.: all end in -**ron**; the ending of -**ar** verbs keeps the vowel of the infinitive (-**a**-); the endings of -**er** and -**ir** verbs change to -**ie**-

2. Irregular verbs

Many verbs are irregular in the preterite and have to be learned individually. Some of them, however, fall into a pattern based on irregularities in their stem, their endings, or both. Here are examples of verbs with irregular stems (the vowel of the stem changes to "u") and the irregular preterite endings added to all **u** stem preterites.

INFINITIVE: estar *(to be)*	saber *(to know)*	tener *(to have)*
STEM: estuv-	sup-	tuv-
estuve estuvimos	supe supimos	tuve tuvimos
estuviste estuvisteis	supiste supisteis	tuviste tuvisteis
estuvo estuvieron	supo supieron	tuvo tuvieron

Look for similarities and differences between these endings for **u** stem verbs and the regular preterite endings above under 1.

Flashcards

On your verb cards add any irregular preterite stems and/or endings.

Practice

1. Sort out some verbs with regular preterite endings.
   - Look at the Spanish side. Write (on a separate piece of paper) or say out loud sentences putting the verb in the preterite tense.
   - Look at the English side. Write (on a separate piece of paper) or say out loud Spanish sentences putting the verb in the preterite tense.

2. Sort out all the verbs with irregular preterite stems and/or endings. Repeat the two steps under No. 1 above.

3. Mix the group of verbs that are regular and irregular in the preterite. Repeat the two steps under No. 1 above.

WHAT IS A PARTICIPLE?

A **PARTICIPLE** is a form of a verb that can be used   1
in one of two ways: with an auxiliary verb to indicate
certain tenses or as an adjective to describe something.

> He *has closed* the door.
> auxiliary + participle → past tense

> He heard me through the *closed* door.
> participle describing *door* → adjective

There are two types of participles: the present participle
and the past participle.   10

PRESENT PARTICIPLE
IN ENGLISH

The present participle is easy to recognize because it is the
-ing form of the verb: *working, studying, dancing, playing.*

The present participle has two primary uses:

1. as the main verb in compound tenses with the auxiliary verb *to be* to indicate a progressive tense (see *What
   are Auxiliary Verbs?*, p. 50 and *What are the Progressive
   Tenses?*, p. 76)   20

> She *is writing* a report with her new computer.
> present progressive of *to write*

> They *were sleeping.*
> past progressive of *to sleep*

2. as an adjective (see *What is an Adjective?*, p. 109)

> A pen is a *writing* instrument.
> describes the noun *instrument*
>   30
> He woke the *sleeping* child.
> describes the noun *child*

IN SPANISH

The present participle can be regular or irregular. Here are
the endings of regular verbs:

- **-ar** verbs add **-ando** to the stem (see p. 45)
- **-er** and **-ir** verbs add **-iendo** to the stem

The **-ndo** of the Spanish participle corresponds to the -*ing* of the English present participle.

Here are examples of regular present participles:

INFINITIVE	STEM	PRESENT PARTICIPLE
cant**ar**	cant-	cant**ando**
com**er**	com-	com**iendo**
viv**ir**	viv-	viv**iendo**

There are some irregular forms that you will have to memorize individually. The present participle is used primarily in the formation of the progressive tenses (see *What are the Progressive Tenses?*, p. 76).

CAREFUL — Never assume that an English word ending in -*ing* will translate by its Spanish counterpart in **-ndo**.

PAST PARTICIPLE
IN ENGLISH

The past participle is formed in several ways. It is the form of the verb that follows *I have*: *I have **spoken**, I have **written**, I have **walked**.*

The past participle has two primary uses:

1. as the main verb in compound tenses with the auxiliary verb *to have*

> I *have written* all that I have to say.
> present perfect of *to write*

> He *had*n't *spoken* to me since our quarrel.
> past perfect of *to speak*

2. as an adjective

> Is the *written* word more important than the *spoken* word?
> describes the noun *word*   describes the noun *word*

IN SPANISH

The past participle can be regular or irregular. Here are the endings of regular verbs:

- **-ar** verbs add **-ado** to the stem
- **-er** and **-ir** verbs add **-ido** to the stem

The **-do** of the Spanish participle often corresponds to the -*ed* of the English past participle.

Here are examples of regular past participles:

INFINITIVE	STEM	PAST PARTICIPLE
cant**ar**	cant-	cant**ado**
com**er**	com-	◦ com**ido**
viv**ir**	viv-	viv**ido**

80

There are some irregular forms that you will have to memorize individually.

As in English, the past participle can be used as the main verb of a compound tense or as an adjective.

1. as the main verb in compound tenses with the auxiliary verb **haber** *(to have)* to indicate a perfect tense (see 90 *What are the Perfect Tenses?*, p. 91)

> Los estudiantes **han terminado** la lección.
> *The students **have finished** the lesson.*

2. as an adjective that agrees with the noun it modifies in gender and number

> *the **closed** door*
>> *Closed* modifies the noun *door*. Since **la puerta** *(door)* is feminine singular, the word for *closed* must be feminine singular. The participle must end with the letter **-a**.
>
> la puerta **cerrada**

100

> *the **stolen** cars*
>> *Stolen* modifies the noun *cars*. Since **los coches** *(cars)* is masculine plural, the word for *stolen* must be masculine plural. The participle must end with the letters **-os**.
>
> los coches **robados**

✎ **REVIEW**

Identify the verb forms in italics by circling: present participle (P) or past participle (PP).

1. At 10:00 p.m. John was *watching* TV.

> P   PP

2. We had already *gone* when Tom called.

> P   PP

3. An antique dealer near our house fixes *broken* china.

> P   PP

4. Mary is *studying* in the library right now.

> P   PP

CHAPTER

21

WHAT ARE THE PROGRESSIVE TENSES?

The **PROGRESSIVE TENSES** are used to talk about actions that are in progress at a specific moment in time; they emphasize the moment that an action takes place.

John *is talking* on the phone.

present progressive:
emphasizes that the action is taking place right now

We *were trying* to start the car.

past progressive:
emphasizes that the action was taking place at a specific time in the past

IN ENGLISH

The progressive tenses are made up of the auxiliary verb *to be* + the present participle of the main verb (see *What is a Participle?*, p. 73).

We *are leaving* right now.

present participle of
main verb *to leave*
present tense of *to be*

At that moment John *was washing* his car.

present participle of
main verb *to wash*
past tense of *to be*

Notice that it is the tense of the auxiliary verb *to be* that indicates when the action of the main verb takes place.

we *are* studying

present tense of *to be* → present progressive

we *were* studying

past tense of *to be* → past progressive

IN SPANISH

The progressive tenses are made up of the auxiliary verb **estar** *(to be)* + the present participle of the main verb. All the tenses in Spanish have a progressive form. In this section we shall only look at the present progressive.

The present progressive is made up of the present tense of **estar** + the present participle of the main verb.

Estamos saliendo ahora mismo.

present tense | present participle
of **estar** | of **salir** *(to leave)*

*We **are leaving** right now.*

¿**Estás comiendo** ahora?

present tense | present participle
of **estar** | of **comer** *(to eat)*

*Are you **eating** now?*

USE OF THE PROGRESSIVE TENSES

The progressive tenses are used far more frequently in English than in Spanish.

In English, the progressive tenses are used for habitual actions, to state general truths, or to indicate that an action is happening at a specific moment (see *What is the Present Tense?*, p. 67).

In Spanish, the progressive tenses are only used for emphasis, for instance, to emphasize that an action is taking place at a particular moment, as opposed to another time, or to stress the continuity of an action. Where English uses the present progressive tense, Spanish often uses the present tense.

*John, what **are you studying** in school?*

English present progressive → Spanish present: **estudias**
You are asking what John is studying in general over a period of time.

*John, what **are you studying** now?*

English present progressive → Spanish present progressive: **estás estudiando**
The word *now* indicates that you want to know what John is studying at this particular time as opposed to all other times.

*Mary, **are you working** for the government?*

English present progressive → Spanish present: **trabajas**
You are asking where Mary is working in general over a period of time.

*Mary, **are you working** right now?*

English present progressive → Spanish present progressive: **estás trabajando**
The words *right now* indicate that you want to know if Mary is working at this particular time as opposed to all other times.

✎ REVIEW

Indicate whether the Spanish version of the following italicized English verbs would use the present tense (P) or the present progressive (PG).

1. This semester Robert *is studying* physics.   P   PG

2. Children, why *are* you *making* so much noise?   P   PG

3. I can't come to the phone. I *am
   getting ready* to go out.   P   PG

4. My brother *is working* for a computer firm
   in California.   P   PG

5. My brother *is doing* very well.   P   PG

WHAT IS MEANT BY MOOD?

> **MOOD** in the grammatical sense applies to verbs
> and indicates the attitude of the speaker
> toward what he or she is saying.   1

Different moods serve different purposes. For example, verbs that state a fact belong to one mood *(you are studying, you studied)*. The verb form that gives orders belongs to another mood *(Study!)*. Some moods have multiple tenses while others have only one tense.

You should recognize the names of the moods so that you will know what your Spanish textbook is referring to when it uses these terms. You will learn when to use the   10
various moods as you learn verbs and their tenses.

IN ENGLISH

Verbs can be in one of three moods.

1. The **INDICATIVE MOOD** is used to state the action of the verb, that is, to *indicate* facts. This is the most common mood, and most of the verb forms that you use in everyday conversation belong to the indicative mood. The majority of the tenses studied in this handbook belong to the indicative mood: for example, the pre-   20
sent tense (see p. 67), the past tense (see p. 69), and the future tense (see p. 95).

> Robert *studies* Spanish.
> present indicative

> Anita *was* here.
> past indicative

> They *will arrive* tomorrow.
> future indicative
>   30

2. The **IMPERATIVE MOOD** is used to give commands or orders (see *What is the Imperative?*, p. 86). This mood is not divided into tenses.

> Robert, *study* Spanish now!
> Anita, *be* home on time!

3. The SUBJUNCTIVE MOOD is used to express an attitude or
feeling toward the action of the verb; it is *subjective*
about it (see *What is the Subjunctive?*, p. 81). In English
this mood is not divided into tenses.

40

> The school requires that students *study* Spanish.
> I wish that Anita *were* here.
> The teacher recommends that he *do* his homework.

IN SPANISH

The Spanish language identifies two moods: the indicative
and the subjunctive.

1. The INDICATIVE MOOD, as in English, is the most common
and most of the tenses you will learn belong to this
mood.

50

2. The SUBJUNCTIVE MOOD is used much more frequently in
Spanish than in English. The Spanish subjunctive has
four tenses: present, imperfect, present perfect, and past
perfect (also called the pluperfect). In addition, most
imperative or command forms are also present subjunctive forms. Textbooks will use the term "present subjunctive" to distinguish that tense from the "present
indicative."

When there is no reference to mood, the verb belongs to
the most common mood, the indicative.

WHAT IS THE SUBJUNCTIVE?

The **SUBJUNCTIVE** is a mood used to express a wish, hope, uncertainty or other similar attitudes toward a fact or an idea. Since it stresses the subject's feelings about the fact or idea, it is usually *subjective* about them.

I wish he *were* here.
subject's subjunctive
wish

The teacher insisted that the homework *be* neat.
subject's subjunctive
attitude

IN ENGLISH

The subjunctive verb form is difficult to recognize because it is spelled like other tenses of the verb: the dictionary form or the simple past tense.

INDICATIVE	SUBJUNCTIVE
He *reads* a lot.	The course requires that he *read* a lot.
present indicative *to read*	subjunctive (same as dictionary form)
I *am* in Detroit right now.	I wish I *were* in Madrid.
present indicative *to be*	subjunctive (same as past tense)

The subjunctive occurs most commonly in three kinds of sentences.

1. The subjunctive form of the verb *to be* (**were**), is used in the if-clause of hypothetical sentences (see p. 99 in *What is the Conditional?* for an explanation of clauses).

      if-clause   result clause
If I *were* in Europe now, I would go to Madrid.
subjunctive

     result clause   if-clause
John would run faster, if he *were* in shape.
subjunctive

2. The same subjunctive form *were* is used in statements expressing a wish.

> I wish I *were* in Europe right now.
> |
> subjunctive

> I wish she *were* my teacher.
> |
> subjunctive

3. The subjunctive form of any verb is used following expressions that ask, urge, demand, request or express necessity.

> She asked that I *come* to see her.
> |___,___| |
> request   subjunctive same as dictionary form

> It is necessary that you *study* a lot.
> |___,___| |
> demand   subjunctive same as dictionary form

IN SPANISH

The subjunctive mood is used very frequently; unfortunately English usage will rarely help you decide where or how to use it in Spanish. It has many tenses in Spanish; however, in this section we shall only look at the present subjunctive.

Here are examples of verbs and expressions that require that the verb that follows (i.e., the second verb) be in the subjunctive, providing that the first and second verb do not have the same subject. Notice that the first verb or the expression remain in the indicative; it is the second verb that is put in the subjunctive.

- a verb of wishing or wanting

> Quiero que Uds. **estudien** mucho.
> | |
> subject **yo**   subject **Uds.**
> **querer** *(to want)* **estudiar** *(to study)*
> indicative   subjunctive

> *I want you **to study** a lot.*
> (word-for-word: *I want that **you study** a lot*)

- an expression of doubt or uncertainty

> Dudo que Roberto **llegue** hoy.
> | |
> subject **yo**   subject **Roberto**
> **dudar** *(to doubt)* **llegar** *(to arrive)*
> indicative   subjunctive

> *I doubt that Robert **will arrive** today.*
> (word-for-word: *I doubt that Robert **arrives** today*)

■ an impersonal expression (**es** + adjective)

Es posible que **compremos** un coche nuevo.

subject "it"	subject **nosotros**
es + adjective	**comprar** *(to buy)*
indicative	subjunctive

*It is possible that **we will buy** a new car.*
(word-for-word: *It is possible that **we buy** a new car*)

■ a verb of advice or command

Te aconsejo que **comas** muchos vegetales.

subject **yo**	subject **tú**
aconsejar *(to advise)*	**comer** *(to eat)*
indicative	subjunctive

*I advise **you to eat** a lot of vegetables.*
(word-for-word: *I advise that **you eat** a lot of vegetables*)

■ an expression of emotion

Siento que Julio **esté** enfermo.

subject **yo**	subject **él**
sentir *(to be sorry)*	**estar** *(to be)*
indicative	subjunctive

*I am sorry that Julio **is** sick.*

If the first and second verbs have the same subject (Ex. *"I'm sorry I'm late"*) the subjunctive is not required. Consult your textbook.

CAREFUL — The tense and mood of an English verb will rarely indicate if you should use the subjunctive in Spanish. As you can see in the examples above, a variety of English verb forms can require a subjunctive in a Spanish sentence.

■ infinitive

*I want you **to study** a lot.*
Quiero que Uds. **estudien** mucho.

*I advise you **to eat** a lot of vegetables.*
Te aconsejo que **comas** muchos vegetales.

■ future tense

*I doubt that Roberto **will arrive** today.*
Dudo que Roberto **llegue** hoy.

*It is possible that **we will buy** a new car.*
Es posible que **compremos** un coche nuevo.

■ present indicative

*I'm sorry that Julio **is** sick.*
Siento que Julio **esté** enfermo.

✎ REVIEW

Indicate the appropriate mood in Spanish for the verbs in italics:
the indicative mood (I) or subjunctive mood (S) .

1. John wants Mary *to go out* with him.   I   S

2. I'm happy that you *got* a good job.   I   S

3. My mother says that Tom *is* a good student.   I   S

4. The doctor suggests that you *take* two aspirins.   I   S

5. It's important for you *to learn* Spanish.   I   S

6. We doubt that he *won* the lottery.   I   S

7. I know that John *lives* in that house.   I   S

STUDY TIPS — THE SUBJUNCTIVE

Patterns (see *Tips for Learning Word Forms* pp. 3-4 and *Tips for
Learning Vocabulary*, pp. 1-3)
1. Subjunctive stems
   - Regular stems: 1st pers. sing. (**yo** form) of the present indicative
     minus the **–o** ending

		Indicative present 1st pers. sing.	Subjunctive stem
hablar	*to speak*	hablo	habl-
comer	*to eat*	como	com-
escribir	*to write*	escribo	escrib-
tener	*to have*	tengo	teng-
salir	*to leave*	salgo	salg-

   - Irregular stems: To be learned as vocabulary.

2. Endings (see your textbook and *Study Tips – Verb Conjugations*, p. 48)
   - **-ar** verbs use the present indicative endings for **–er, -ir** verbs

hablar	hable	hablemos
	hables	habléis
	hable	hablen

   - **-er** and **–ir** verbs use the present indicative endings for **–ar** verbs

tener	tenga	tengamos	**salir**	salga	salgamos
	tengas	tengáis		salgas	salgáis
	tenga	tengan		salga	salgan

In summary, the present subjunctive is identifiable from the present indicative by the "traded" endings: verbs with "**a**" in the
indicative endings have an "**e**" in the subjunctive endings and
verbs with an "**e**" or "**i**" in the indicative endings have an "**a**" in
the subjunctive endings.

Flashcards

On your verb cards, add the irregular subjunctive stem, if there is one.

ir	*to go*
vay- (subjunctive stem)	
saber	*to know*
sep- (subjunctive stem)	

On your verb cards, indicate those verbs that require that the verb of the second clause be in the subjunctive.

querer + subj.	*to want, to wish*
recomendar + subj.	*to recommend*

Practice

A. LEARNING THE SUBJUNCTIVE FORMS

1. Sort out some verbs with regular subjunctive stems.
   - Look at the Spanish side. Write (on a separate piece of paper) or say out loud sentences putting the verb in the present subjunctive.
   - Look at the English side. Write (on a separate piece of paper) or say out loud Spanish sentences putting the verb in the present subjunctive.
2. Sort out the verbs with irregular subjunctive stems. Repeat the two steps under No. 1 above.
3. Mix the group of verbs with regular and irregular subjunctive stems. Repeat the two steps under No. 1 above.
4. Using the group of verbs with regular and irregular subjunctive stems, write (on a separate piece of paper) or say out loud the present indicative forms followed by the present subjunctive forms. This will help you to remember what distinguishes one from the other.

B. LEARNING TO USE THE SUBJUNCTIVE

1. Learn the verbs and expressions that require that the verb which follows be put in the subjunctive.
2. Sort out some verbs that require the use of the subjunctive in the second clause of the sentence.
   - Look at the Spanish side. Write (on a separate piece of paper) or say out loud sentences with two clauses, the first verb requiring the subjunctive in the second clause.
   - Look at the English side. Write (on a separate piece of paper) or say out loud Spanish sentences with two clauses, the first verb requiring the subjunctive in the second clause.

querer *to want, to wish*
Quiero que Juan **estudie** mucho. *I want Juan **to study** a lot.*

dudar *to doubt*
Dudo que Juan **hable** inglés. *I doubt that Juan **speaks** English.*

WHAT IS THE IMPERATIVE?

The IMPERATIVE is used to give someone an order.

The AFFIRMATIVE IMPERATIVE is an order to do something.

Come here!

The NEGATIVE IMPERATIVE is an order not to do something.

Don't come here!

IN ENGLISH

There are two types of commands, depending on who is told to do, or not to do, something.

1. "YOU" **COMMAND** — When an order is given to one or more persons, the dictionary form of the verb is used.

AFFIRMATIVE IMPERATIVE	NEGATIVE IMPERATIVE
Answer the phone.	*Don't answer* the phone.
Clean your room.	*Don't clean* your room.
Speak softly.	*Don't speak* softly.

2. "WE" **COMMAND** — When an order is given to oneself as well as to others, the phrase "let's" (a contraction of *let us*) is used + the dictionary form of the verb.

AFFIRMATIVE IMPERATIVE	NEGATIVE IMPERATIVE
Let's leave.	*Let's not leave.*
Let's go to the movies.	*Let's not go* to the movies.

IN SPANISH

As in English, there are affirmative and negative commands.

1. "YOU" **COMMAND** — There are many forms of the "you" command to distinguish familiar and formal, as well as affirmative and negative.

   ▪ "Tú" **command** — When an order is given to a person to whom you say **tú**.

   The regular affirmative **tú** command has the same form as the 3rd person singular of the present indicative tense. There are also several irregular forms that you will have to learn individually. The negative **tú** command has the same form as the 2nd person singular of the present subjunctive.

AFFIRMATIVE IMPERATIVE | NEGATIVE IMPERATIVE

Habla.

present indicative
3rd pers. sing.

Speak.

No hables.

present subjunctive
2nd pers. sing.

Don't speak.

Ven aquí.

irregular form

Come here.

No vengas aquí.

present subjunctive
2nd pers. sing.

Don't come here.

- **"Vosostros" command** — When an order is given to two or more persons to whom you say **tú** individually. The **vosotros** command is a familiar plural command and is used only in Spain.

  The affirmative **vosotros** command is formed by dropping the **-r** from the infinitive ending and replacing it with the letter **-d**. The negative **vosotros** command has the same form as the 2nd person plural of the present subjunctive.

AFFIRMATIVE IMPERATIVE | NEGATIVE IMPERATIVE

Venid aquí.

infinitive **venir** *(to come)*
-r → -d

Come here.

No vengáis aquí.

present subjunctive
2nd per. pl.

Don't come here.

Hablad.

infinitive **hablar** *(to speak)*
-r → -d

Speak.

No habláis.

present subjunctive
2nd pers. pl.

Don't speak.

- **"Usted" command** — When an order is given to a person to whom you say **usted**.

  Both the affirmative and negative **usted** commands have the same form as the 3rd person singular of the present subjunctive.

AFFIRMATIVE IMPERATIVE | NEGATIVE IMPERATIVE

Hable.

present subjunctive
3rd pers. sing.

Speak.

No hable.

present subjunctive
3rd pers. sing.

Don't speak.

Venga aquí.
|
present subjunctive
3rd pers. sing.
Come here.

No venga aquí.
|
present subjunctive
3rd pers. sing.
Don't come here.

■ **"Ustedes" command** — IN SPAIN: When an order is given to two or more persons to whom you say **usted** individually. IN LATIN AMERICA: When an order is given to two or more persons to whom you say **tú** or **usted** individually.

Both the affirmative and negative **ustedes** commands have the same form as the 3rd person plural of the present subjunctive.

AFFIRMATIVE IMPERATIVE
Hablen.
|
present subjunctive
3rd pers. pl.
Speak.

NEGATIVE IMPERATIVE
No hablen.
|
present subjunctive
3rd pers. pl.
Don't speak.

Vengan aquí.
|
present subjunctive
3rd pers. pl.
Come here.

No vengan aquí.
|
present subjunctive
3rd pers. pl.
Don't come here.

2. **"WE" COMMAND** — The affirmative and negative **nosotros** commands have the same form as the 1st person plural of the present subjunctive.

AFFIRMATIVE IMPERATIVE
Hablemos.
|
present subjunctive
1st pers. pl.
Let's talk.

NEGATIVE IMPERATIVE
No hablemos.
|
present subjunctive
1st pers. pl.
Let's not talk.

Salgamos.
|
present subjunctive
1st pers. pl.
Let's leave.

No salgamos.
|
present subjunctive
1st pers. pl.
Let's not leave.

Notice that the English phrase *let's* does not translate into Spanish; the command ending is the equivalent of *let's*.

In English and in Spanish the absence of the pronoun in the sentence is a good indication that you are dealing with an imperative and not a present tense (see *What is the Present Tense?*, p. 67).

You answer the phone.
| present

120

Answer the phone.
| imperative

SUMMARY

Here is a chart you can use as a reference for choosing the proper form of the Spanish command.

COMMAND FORMS		
	AFFIRMATIVE	**NEGATIVE**
tú *you*	present **indicative** 3rd pers. sing.	present **subjunctive** 2nd pers. sing.
vosotros *you*	infinitive -r → -d	present **subjunctive** 2nd pers. pl.
usted *you*	present **subjunctive** 3rd pers. sing.	present **subjunctive** 3rd pers. sing.
ustedes *you*	present **subjunctive** 3rd pers. pl.	present **subjunctive** 3rd pers. pl.
nosotros *we*	present **subjunctive** 1st pers. pl.	present **subjunctive** 1st pers. pl.

130

140

✎ REVIEW

A. Change the sentences below to an affirmative command.

1. You must study for the exam.

_____

2. We go to the movies every weekend.

_____

3. You should eat more fruit and vegetables.

_____

B. Change the sentences below to a negative command.

1. You shouldn't sleep in class.

_____

2. You must not work so much.

_____

3. We are not eating out tonight.

_____

Patterns

Look for a pattern in the chart of command forms on p. 89.

1. What is the form used: the present subjunctive, a modified infinitive, or the present indicative?

   ■ The present subjunctive is used for all forms, affirmative and negative, except the affirmative commands of **tú** and **vosotros**.

   ■ A modified infinitive with the final -r replaced by -d is used for the affirmative command of **vosotros**.

   ■ The present indicative is used for the affirmative command of **tú**.

2. What is the person used: the 2nd pers. sing., 3rd pers. sing., or the 1st pers. pl.?

   ■ as usual, **Ud.**, **Uds.** use the 3rd pers. sing. and pl.

   ■ as usual, **nosotros** uses the 1st pers. pl.

   ■ as usual, **tú** uses the 2nd pers. sing., but only for the negative

   ■ unusual, **tú** uses the 3rd pers. sing. for the affirmative

   ■ unusual, **vosotros** uses a modified infinitive which has no person

INFINITIVE: esperar *(to hope)*

	AFFIRMATIVE		NEGATIVE	
(tú)	espera	(IND. 3RD PERS. SING.)	no esperes	(SUBJ. 2ND PERS. SING.)
(vosotros)	esperad	(INF. -R → -D)	no esperéis	(SUBJ. 2ND PERS. PL.)
(Ud.)	espere	(SUBJ. 3RD PERS. SING.)	no espere	(SUBJ. 3RD PERS. SING.)
(Uds.)	esperen	(SUBJ. 3RD PERS. PL.)	no esperen	(SUBJ. 3RD PERS. PL.)
(nosotros)	esperemos	(SUBJ. 1ST PERS. PL.)	no esperemos	(SUBJ. 1ST PERS. PL.)

Flashcards

Since the imperative of a verb has such a variety of forms, it is advisable to write all the forms, negative and affirmative, on your flashcard so that you can review them. Negative forms can be in parentheses after the word "no."

INFINITIVE:	ir *(to go)*	empezar *(to begin)*
(tú)	vé (no vayas)	empieza (no empieces)
(vosotros)	id (no vayáis)	empezad (no empecéis)
(Ud.)	vaya (no vaya)	empiece (no empiece)
(Uds.)	vayan (no vayan)	empiecen (no empiecen)
(nosotros)	vamos (no vayamos)	empecemos (no empecemos)

Practice

1. Sort out the verbs with regular imperative forms.

   ■ Look at the Spanish side. Write (on a separate piece of paper) or say out loud the affirmative and negative command forms in a short sentence.

   ■ Look at the English side. Write (on a separate piece of paper) or say out loud the affirmative and negative **tú** command forms of the equivalent Spanish verb in a sentence.

2. Repeat the above with irregular imperative forms.

WHAT ARE THE PERFECT TENSES?

The PERFECT TENSES are compound verbs made up of the
auxiliary verb *to have* + the past participle of the
main verb (see *What is a Participle?*, p. 73).

> I *have* not *seen* him.
> | |
> auxiliary past participle
> verb   of *to see*

> They *had* already *gone*.
> | |
> auxiliary   past participle
> verb   of *to go*

IN ENGLISH

There are four perfect tenses formed with the auxiliary
verb *to have* + the past participle of the main verb. The
name of each perfect tense is based on the tense used for
the auxiliary verb *to have*.

1. **Present perfect** — *to have* in the present tense + the
   past participle of the main verb (see *What is the Present
   Tense?*, p. 67).

   > I *have eaten*.
   > | |
   > present past participle
   >   of *to eat*

   > The boys *have washed* the car.
   > | |
   >   present past participle
   >   of *to wash*

2. **Past perfect (pluperfect)** — *to have* in the simple past
   (past definite) + the past participle of the main verb
   (see *What is the Past Tense?*, p. 69).

   > I *had eaten* before six.
   > | |
   > simple past participle
   > past   of *to eat*

   > The boys *had washed* the car before the storm.
   > | |
   >   simple past participle
   >   past   of *to wash*

3. **Future perfect** — *to have* in the future tense + the past participle of the main verb (see *What is the Future Tense?*, p. 95).

> I *will have eaten* by six o'clock.
> └──┬──┘ |
> future past participle
>   of *to eat*

> The boys *will have washed* the car by Thursday.
> └──┬──┘ |
> future past participle
>   of *to wash*

4. **Conditional perfect** — *to have* in the conditional + the past participle of the main verb (see *What is the Conditional?*, p. 99).

> I *would have eaten* if I had had the time.
> └──┬──┘ |
> conditional past participle
>   of *to eat*

> John *would have washed* the car if he had been here.
> └──┬──┘ |
> conditional past participle
>   of *to wash*

IN SPANISH

The perfect tenses are made up of a form of the auxiliary verb **haber** *(to have)* + the past participle of the main verb. In Spanish there are several perfect tenses: four perfect tenses in the indicative mood (see *What is Meant by Mood?*, p. 79) and two in the subjunctive (see *What is the Subjunctive?*, p. 81). As in English, the name of the tense is based on the tense of the auxiliary verb **haber**.

We are listing the various perfect tenses here so that you can see the pattern that they follow. The perfect tenses are not always used in the same way in Spanish as in English. Consult your Spanish textbook in order to learn to use them properly.

SPANISH PERFECT TENSES IN THE INDICATIVE MOOD

1. **Present perfect** (perfecto) — **haber** in the present tense + the past participle of the main verb. Generally the Spanish present perfect is used in the same way as the present perfect in English.

> **He comido.**
> *I have eaten.*

> Los chicos **han lavado** el coche.
> *The boys **have washed** the car.*

2. **Past perfect or Pluperfect** (pluscuamperfecto) — **haber** in the imperfect + the past participle of the main verb. The past perfect is used to express an action completed in the past before some other past action or event. Generally, the Spanish past perfect is used the same way as the past perfect in English.

> **Había comido** antes de las seis.
> *I had eaten before six o'clock.*

> Los chicos **habían lavado** el coche antes de la tempestad.
> *The boys had washed the car before the storm.*

3. **Future perfect** (futuro perfecto) — **haber** in the future + the past participle of the main verb. Generally, the Spanish future perfect is used in the same way as the future perfect in English.

> **Habré comido** para las seis.
> *I will have eaten by six o'clock.*

> Los chicos **habrán lavado** el coche para el jueves.
> *The boys will have washed the car by Thursday.*

4. **Conditional perfect** (condicional perfecto) — **haber** in the conditional + the past participle of the main verb.

> **Habría comido** si hubiera tenido tiempo.
> *I would have eaten if I had had time.*

> Los chicos **habrían lavado** el coche si hubieran estado aquí.
> *The boys would have washed the car if they had been here.*

SPANISH PERFECT TENSES IN THE SUBJUNCTIVE

1. **Present perfect subjunctive** (perfecto del subjuntivo) — **haber** in the present subjunctive + the past participle of the main verb. This tense is really just a present perfect used when a subjunctive is required.

> *He hopes that **they have arrived**.*
> requires that present perfect subjunctive → **hayan llegado**
> the following
> verb be in the subjunctive

2. **Pluperfect subjunctive** (pluscuamperfecto del subjuntivo) — **haber** in the imperfect subjunctive + the past participle of the main verb.

> *He hoped that **they had arrived**.*
> requires that pluperfect subjunctive → **hubieran llegado**
> the following
> verb be in the subjunctive

✎ REVIEW

Indicate the tense of the verb in italics by circling present perfect (P), past perfect (PP), future perfect (FP) or conditional perfect (CP).

1. We *had* already *gone*
   when Teresa arrived.　　　　　　　　　P　　PP　　FP　　CP

2. Barbara *hasn't left* yet.　　　　　　　P　　PP　　FP　　CP

3. I *will have graduated*
   by next summer.　　　　　　　　　　　P　　PP　　FP　　CP

4. We *would have studied* more　　　　　P　　PP　　FP　　CP

   if we *had remembered* the exam.　　　P　　PP　　FP　　CP

5. *Have* you *seen* my new car?　　　　　P　　PP　　FP　　CP

STUDY TIPS — THE PERFECT TENSES

Patterns (see *Tips for Learning Word Forms*, pp. 3-4 and *Tips for Learning Vocabulary*, pp. 1-3)

1. Review the conjugation of **haber** *(to have)* in the tenses you will need to form the various perfect tenses (see pp. 92-93).
   - present: he, has, ha, hemos, habéis, han
   - imperfect: había, habías, había, habíamos, habíais, habían
   - future: habré, habrás, habrá, habremos, habréis, habrán
   - conditional: habría, habrías, habría, habríamos, habríais, habrían

2. Review the formation of past participles (see pp. 74-5)
   - regular past participle: -**ar** add -**ado** to the stem, -**er** and -**ir** add -**ido**
   - irregular past participle: To be learned as vocabulary.

Flashcards

Add to the Spanish side of your verb flashcards the irregular past participle, if there is one.

Practice

PRESENT PERFECT TENSE

1. Sort out some verbs with regular past participles.
   - Look at the Spanish side. Write (on a separate piece of paper) or say out loud sentences putting the verb into the present perfect tense.
   - Look at the English side. Write (on a separate piece of paper) or say out loud Spanish sentences putting the verb into the present perfect tense.

2. Sort out the verbs with irregular past participles. Follow the steps under No. 1 above.

Follow the steps above to practice the past perfect (pluperfect), future perfect, and conditional perfect tenses.

WHAT IS THE FUTURE TENSE?

The **FUTURE TENSE** indicates that an action will take place some time in the future.   1

I *will return* the book as soon as I've read it.
    └─┬─┘
    future

IN ENGLISH

The future tense is formed with the auxiliary words *will* or *shall* + the dictionary form of the main verb. Note that *shall* is used in formal English (and British English) and *will* occurs in everyday language. In conversation *shall* and *will* are often shortened to *'ll*.   10

> Paul and Mary *will do* their homework tomorrow.
> *I'll leave* tonight.

IN SPANISH

You do not need an auxiliary to show that an action will take place. The future tense is indicated by a simple tense.

Regular verbs use the infinitive as a stem for the future tense.

Infinitive	Stem	
visitar	visitar-	*to visit*
comer	comer-	*to eat*
vivir	vivir-	*to live*

   20

Irregular verbs have irregular future stems that you will have to memorize individually. Your textbook will list irregular future verb stems and give you the endings to be added in order to form the future tense.

SUBSTITUTE FOR THE FUTURE TENSE

In English and in Spanish an action that will occur some time in the future can also be expressed without using the future tense itself, but with a construction called the **IMMEDIATE FUTURE**.   30

IN ENGLISH

The immediate future is expressed with the verb *to go* in the present progressive tense + the infinitive of the main verb: *I am going to travel, she is going to dance.*

similar meaning

I am going to travel.   *I will travel.*

present progressive   future tense
of *to go* + infinitive

IN SPANISH

The same construction exists in Spanish; it is formed with the verb **ir** *(to go)* in the present tense + **a** + the infinitive of the main verb: **voy a viajar** *(I'm going to travel)*, **ella va a bailar** *(she's going to dance)*.

Look at the difference between the forms of the two constructions.

similar meaning

Voy a estudiar.   **Estudiaré.**

present of **ir** +   future tense
a + infinitive

I am going to study.   *I will study.*

present progressive   future tense
of *to go* + infinitive

CAREFUL — Note that the "**a**" has no English equivalent; it must appear in the Spanish sentence, however.

FUTURE OF PROBABILITY

In addition to expressing an action that will take place in the future, the future tense in Spanish can be used to express a probable fact, what the speaker feels is probably true. This is called the FUTURE OF PROBABILITY.

IN ENGLISH

The idea of probability is expressed with words such as *must, probably, wonder.*

My keys *must* be around here.
My keys are *probably* around here.
I *wonder* if my keys are around here.

IN SPANISH

It is not necessary to use the words *must, probably,* or *wonder* to express probable facts; the main verb is simply put into the future tense.

I wonder what time it is.

present tense   main verb → present tense

¿Qué hora **será**?

main verb future tense

It's probably 4:00 o'clock.
|
main verb *is* → present tense
Serán las cuatro.
|
main verb → future tense

*I can't find my book. John **must have** it.*
|
main verb → infinitive
No puedo encontrar mi libro. Juan lo **tendrá**.
|
main verb → future tense

✎ REVIEW

Circle the verbs in the following sentences.
- On the line provided, write the dictionary form of the English verb you would put in the future tense in Spanish.

DICTIONARY FORM

1. The students will study for the exam. _____

2. I'll clean my room later. _____

3. Shall we leave? _____

4. I won't finish until tomorrow. _____

5. Will she be here by 9:00? _____

STUDY TIPS — THE FUTURE TENSE

Patterns

1. Future stems (see *Tips for Learning Word Forms*, pp. 3-4 and *Tips for Learning Vocabulary*, pp. 1-3)

   Regular stems: The infinitive form is the stem.
   Irregular stems: Stems must be learned as vocabulary.

2. Endings: All the verbs, regardless if they have a regular or an irregular stem, add the same endings.

INFINITIVE:	hablar	salir	
STEM:	hablar- *(reg.)*	saldr- *(irreg.)*	
hablaré	hablaremos	saldré	saldremos
hablarás	hablaréis	saldrás	saldéis
hablará	hablarán	saldrá	saldrán

   What pattern do you see?
   - all forms have an accent, except the 1st pers. pl. form
   - in the ending, the vowel -e is used three times, in the 1st pers. sing. and the 1st and 2nd pers. pl.; the vowel -a is also used three times, in the 2nd and 3rd pers. sing. and the 3rd pers. pl.

Flashcards

On your verb card add the irregular future stem, if there is one. NOTE: The future stem will also be the stem for the conditional (see *What is the Conditional?*, p. 99).

decir	*to say, to tell*
dir-	(stem: future/conditional
salir	*to leave*
saldr-	(stem: future/conditional

Practice

1. Sort out some verbs with regular future stems.

   - Look at the Spanish side of the card. Write (on a separate piece of paper) or say out loud sentences putting the verb in the future tense.
   - Look at the English side. Write (on a separate piece of paper) or say out loud Spanish sentences putting the verb in the future tense.

2. Sort out the verbs with irregular future stems. Repeat the two steps under No. 1 above.

3. Mix the group of verbs with regular and irregular stems. Repeat the two steps under No. 1 above.

WHAT IS THE CONDITIONAL?

The **CONDITIONAL** forms of a verb get their name because they are primarily used in sentences that imply a condition.

> If I were offered the job, I *would take* it.
>   condition   conditional form of the verb

The conditional has a present and past tense called the conditional (present) and the conditional perfect (past).

CONDITIONAL (PRESENT)
IN ENGLISH

The conditional is a compound tense made up of the auxiliary word **would** + the dictionary form of the main verb: I *would eat*.

The conditional is used in the following ways:

1. as a polite form with *like* and in polite requests

> I *would like* to eat.
> More polite than "I want to eat."

> *Would* you please close the door.
> "Please close the door" is softened by the use of *would*.

2. in the result clause of a hypothetical statement

A **HYPOTHETICAL STATEMENT** includes a condition that does not exist at the present time, but could possibly become a reality one day.

>   condition   result clause
> If Paul had money, he *would buy* a house.
> subject verb   subject   verb in the conditional

The above statement is hypothetical because Paul does not have money at the present time; but there is the possibility that he will have money someday and, therefore, be able to buy a house.

A **CLAUSE** is a part of a sentence composed of a group of words containing a subject and a verb. In a hypothetical statement there are two types of clauses: the *if* clause and the result clause.

- **IF CLAUSE** — expresses the condition which must be met. In the above example: "If Paul had money...."
- **RESULT CLAUSE** — expresses the result if the condition is met. In the above example: "he would buy a house."

3. in an indirect statement to express a future-in-the-past

An **INDIRECT STATEMENT** repeats, or reports, but does not quote, someone's words, as opposed to a **DIRECT STATEMENT** which is a word-for-word quotation of what someone said. In written form a direct statement is always between quotation marks.

DIRECT STATEMENT   Paul said: *"Mary will come."*
                                            1   2
                                          past   future

INDIRECT STATEMENT   Paul said *Mary would come.*
                                          1   2
                                        past   present conditional

In the direct statement, action 2 is a quotation in the future tense. In an indirect statement, action 2 is called a **FUTURE-IN-THE-PAST** because it takes place in the past after another action in the past.

IN SPANISH

Unlike English where the conditional is a compound tense, in Spanish, the conditional is a simple tense formed with the future stem (see p. 95) + the endings of the imperfect tense for **-er** and **-ir** verbs (see your textbook).

FUTURE STEM	CONDITIONAL	
hablar-	hablaría	*I would speak*
comer-	comería	*I would eat*
vivir-	viviría	*I would live*
pondr-	pondría	*I would put*
har-	haría	*I would do*

The conditional is used in the same ways as in English:

1. as a polite form or in polite requests

Querría un vaso de agua.
|
conditional
I would like a glass of water.

¿**Podría** Ud. cerrar la puerta, por favor?
|
conditional
Would you close the door, please?

2. in the result clause of a hypothetical statement   80

> Si tuviera mucho dinero, **compraría** una casa grande.
> |
> conditional
> *If I had a lot of money, **I would buy** a big house.*

3. in an indirect statement to express a future-in-the-past

> Dijo que **vendría.**
> |
> conditional
> *He said (that) **he would come.***

> Sabía que **llovería** esta noche.   90
> |
> conditional
> *I knew (that) **it would rain** this evening.*

CONDITIONAL PERFECT (PAST)
IN ENGLISH

The conditional perfect is a compound tense made up of the auxiliary *would have* + past participle of the main verb: *I would have eaten, he would have come.*

The conditional perfect is used in the result clause of contrary-to-fact statements. A statement is CONSTRARY-TO-   100
FACT when a condition was not met in the past and therefore the result was not accomplished.

> *if* clause   result clause
> If I had had money, I *would have bought* a new house.

The statement above is contrary-to-fact because the person speaking didn't have money in the past and therefore did not buy a new house.

> He *would have spoken* if he had known the truth.   110
> Contrary-to-fact: He did not speak
> because he didn't know the truth.

> If you had called us, we *would have come.*
> Contrary-to-fact: We did not come
> because you didn't call us.

IN SPANISH

The conditional perfect is a compound tense made up of the auxiliary verb **haber** *(to have)* in the conditional tense + the past participle of the main verb: **habría hablado** *(I would have spoken)*. As in English, statements using the   120
conditional perfect are contrary-to-fact.

Si hubieran estudiado más, **habrían recibido** mejores notas.

conditional perfect

*If they had studied more, **they would have received** better grades.*

SEQUENCE OF TENSES

Let us look at examples of hypothetical and contrary-to-fact statements so that you learn to use the appropriate tense in each clause.

Hypothetical and contrary-to-fact statements are easy to recognize because they are made up of two clauses:

- the IF CLAUSE (the clause that starts with *if,* **si** in Spanish)
- the RESULT CLAUSE

The sequence of tenses is sometimes the same in both English and Spanish. If you have difficulty recognizing tenses, just apply these three rules.

"IF" CLAUSE → PRESENT   RESULT CLAUSE → FUTURE

---

*If I **have** time, I **will go** to the party.*

present   future

Si **tengo** tiempo, **iré** a la fiesta.

present   future

"IF" CLAUSE → PAST (English)   RESULT CLAUSE → CONDITIONAL
IMPERFECT SUBJUNCTIVE (Spanish)

---

*If I **had** more time, I **would go** to the party.*

past   conditional

Si **tuviera** más tiempo, **iría** a la fiesta.

imperfect   conditional
subjunctive

"IF" CLAUSE → PAST PERFECT (English)   RESULT CLAUSE → CONDITIONAL PERFECT
PLUPERFECT SUBJUNCTIVE (Spanish)

---

*If I **had had** more time, I **would have gone** to the party.*

past perfect   conditional perfect

Si **hubiera tenido** más tiempo, **habría ido** a la fiesta.

pluperfect   conditional perfect
subjunctive

CAREFUL — In English and in Spanish, the *if clause* can come before or after the result clause. The tense of a clause remains the same regardless of the order of the clauses.

*I **would have gone** to the party, if **I had had** more time.*
conditional perfect   past perfect   170

Habría ido a la fiesta, si **hubiera tenido** más tiempo.
conditional perfect   pluperfect
subjunctive

✎ REVIEW

Write the tense you would use in Spanish for each of the italicized verbs below: present (P), preterite (PT), future (F), conditional (C), conditional perfect (CP), imperfect subjunctive (IS), or the pluperfect subjunctive (PS).

1. I *know* the children *will enjoy* that movie.

   _____   _____

2. We *would go* to Spain if we *had* the money.

   _____   _____

3. I *would like* some more meat, please.

   _____

4. If it *rains*, they *won't have* the picnic.

   _____   _____

5. My parents *wrote* that they *would come* in July.

   _____   _____

6. If I *had known* you were coming, I *wouldn't have left*.

   _____   _____

CHAPTER

WHAT IS MEANT BY ACTIVE AND PASSIVE VOICE?

VOICE in the grammatical sense refers to the relationship between the verb and its subject. There are two voices, the **ACTIVE VOICE** and the **PASSIVE VOICE**.

ACTIVE VOICE — A sentence is said to be in the active voice when the subject is the performer of the action of the verb. In this instance, the verb is called an **ACTIVE VERB**.

The teacher prepares the exam.
　　　　S　　　V　　　　DO

Paul ate an apple.
　S　V　　DO

Lightning has struck the tree.
　　S　　　　V　　　　DO

In these examples the subject (S) performs the action of the verb (V) and the direct object (DO) is the receiver of the action (see *What is a Subject?,* p. 29 and *What are Objects?*, p. 140).

PASSIVE VOICE — A sentence is said to be in the passive voice when the subject is the receiver of the action of the verb. In this instance, the verb is called a **PASSIVE VERB**.

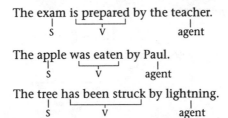

In these examples, the subject is the receiver of the action of the verb. The performer of the action, if it is mentioned, is introduced by the word "by" and is called the **AGENT**.

IN ENGLISH

The passive voice is expressed by the verb *to be* conjugated in the appropriate tense + the past participle of the main verb (see *What is a Participle?*, p. 73). The tense of the passive sentence is indicated by the tense of the verb *to be*.

The exam *is prepared* by the teacher.

present

The exam *was prepared* by the teacher.

past

The exam *will be prepared* by the teacher.

future

IN SPANISH

As in English, a passive verb can be expressed by the auxiliary verb **ser** *(to be)* conjugated in the appropriate tense + the past participle of the main verb. The tense of the passive sentence is indicated by the tense of the verb **ser**.

El examen **es** preparado por el profesor.

present
The exam is prepared by the teacher.

El examen **fue** preparado por el profesor.

past
The exam has been (was) prepared by the teacher.

El examen **será** preparado por el profesor.

future
The exam will be prepared by the teacher.

In the passive voice formed with **ser** all past participles agree in gender and number with the subject.

Esas **cartas** fueron **escritas** por el profesor.

fem. pl.   fem. pl.
Those letters were written by the teacher.

MAKING AN ACTIVE SENTENCE PASSIVE

The steps to change an active sentence to a passive sentence are the same in English and in Spanish.

1. The direct object of the active sentence is made the subject of the passive sentence.

ACTIVE   The teacher prepares *the exam.*

direct object

PASSIVE   *The exam* is prepared by the teacher.

subject

2. The tense of the verb of the active sentence is reflected in the tense of the verb *to be* in the passive sentence.

ACTIVE   The teacher *prepares* the exam.
                           present

PASSIVE   The exam *is* prepared by the teacher.
                           present

ACTIVE   The teacher *prepared* the exam.
                           past

PASSIVE   The exam *was* prepared by the teacher.
                           past

ACTIVE   The teacher *will* prepare the exam.
                           future

PASSIVE   The exam *will be* prepared by the teacher.
                           future

3. The subject of the active sentence is made the agent of the passive sentence introduced with *by*.

ACTIVE   *The teacher* prepares the exam.
                           subject

PASSIVE   The exam is prepared *by the teacher*.
                           agent

AVOIDING THE PASSIVE VOICE IN SPANISH

Although Spanish has a passive voice, whenever possible Spanish speakers try to avoid it by replacing it with an active construction. This is particularly true for general statements when we don't know who is doing the action.

English *is spoken* in many countries.
We don't know who is speaking.

The New York Times *is sold* here.
We don't know who is selling.

There are two ways a passive sentence can be avoided in Spanish.

1. using the "**se** construction" — The word **se** corresponds to the English indefinite pronoun *one* used in a general sense as in the sentence "*One* should eat when *one* is hungry." Spanish often makes *one* the subject of an active sentence, even in cases where English speakers would never use such a construction.

*English **is spoken** in many countries.*

"one speaks"

Se habla inglés en muchos países.

*The New York Times **is sold** here.*

"one sells"

Se vende el New York Times aquí.

2. using the 3ʳᵈ person plural of the verb — The main verb of the sentence is changed from the English passive voice to the equivalent Spanish verb in the 3ʳᵈ person plural. (The "they" corresponds to a general subject, such as *"They* say Mexico is very interesting.") The subject of the English sentence becomes the direct object in the Spanish sentence.

*English **is spoken** in many countries.*

subject + passive verb

*"**they speak** English"*

3ʳᵈ pers. pl. + active verb + DO

Hablan inglés en muchos países.

*The New York Times **is sold** here.*

subject + passive verb

*"**they sell** the New York Times"*

3ʳᵈ pers. pl. + active verb + DO

Venden el New York Times aquí.

CAREFUL — Make sure you distinguish between the auxiliary **haber** *(to have)* + the past participle used to form a past tense in the active voice (see *What are the Perfect Tenses?*, p. 91) and **ser** *(to be)* + the past participle used to form a passive sentence. For example, **ha cerrado** is a past tense of the verb **cerrar** *(to close)* in the active voice and **fue cerrado** is a past tense in the passive voice. As you can see in the following examples, the same changes occur in English.

ACTIVE *The teacher **has** prepared the exam.*

auxiliary *to have* → past (present perfect)

PASSIVE *The exam **was** prepared by the teacher.*

auxiliary *to be* → past

ACTIVE   El profesor **ha** escrito el examen.

▼   auxiliary **haber** *(to have)* → past (present perfect)

PASSIVE   El examen **fue** escrito por el profesor.

          auxiliary **ser** *(to be)* → past

✎ REVIEW

Underline the subjects in the sentences below.
- Circle the performer of the action.
- Identify each sentence as active (Ac) or passive (Pᴀ).
- Identify the tense of the verb: past (PP), present (P), future (F).

1. The cow jumped over the moon.   Ac   Pᴀ   PP   P   F

2. The bill was paid by Bob's parents.   Ac   Pᴀ   PP   P   F

3. The bank transfers the money.   Ac   Pᴀ   PP   P   F

4. Everyone will be going away
   during August.   Ac   Pᴀ   PP   P   F

5. The spring break will be enjoyed
   by all.   Ac   Pᴀ   PP   P   F

WHAT IS AN ADJECTIVE?

An **ADJECTIVE** is a word that describes a noun or a pronoun.   1
There are different types of adjectives which
are classified according to the way
they describe a noun or pronoun.

DESCRIPTIVE ADJECTIVE — A descriptive adjective indicates a
quality; it tells what kind of noun it is (see p. 110).

> She read an *interesting* book.
> He has *brown* eyes.

POSSESSIVE ADJECTIVE— A possessive adjective shows possession; it tells whose noun it is (see p. 118).   10

> *His* book is lost.
> *Our* parents are away.

INTERROGATIVE ADJECTIVE — An interrogative adjective asks a
question about a noun (see p. 126).

> *What* book is lost?
> *Which* book did you read?

DEMONSTRATIVE ADJECTIVE — A demonstrative adjective
points out a noun (see p. 129).

> *This* teacher is excellent.   20
> *That* question is very appropriate.

IN ENGLISH

English adjectives usually do not change their form,
regardless of the noun or pronouns described.

IN SPANISH

The principal difference between English and Spanish
adjectives is that while in English adjectives do not
change their form, in Spanish adjectives change in order
to agree in gender and number with the noun or pronoun   30
they modify.

STUDY TIPS — DESCRIPTIVE ADJECTIVES (SEE P. 113)

STUDY TIPS — POSSESSIVE ADJECTIVES (SEE P. 125)

CHAPTER

WHAT IS A DESCRIPTIVE ADJECTIVE?

A **DESCRIPTIVE ADJECTIVE** is a word that indicates a quality of a noun or pronoun. As the name implies, it *describes* the noun or pronoun.

The book is *interesting*.
noun   descriptive
described   adjective

IN ENGLISH

A descriptive adjective does not change form, regardless of the noun or pronoun it modifies.

The students are *intelligent*.
She is an *intelligent* person.

The form of the adjective *intelligent* remains the same although the persons described are different in number (*students* is plural and *person* is singular).

Descriptive adjectives are divided into two groups depending on how they are connected to the noun they modify.

1. A **PREDICATE ADJECTIVE** is connected to the noun it describes, always the subject of the sentence, by **LINKING VERBS** such as *to be, to feel, to look*.

The children are *good*.
noun   linking predicate
described   verb   adjective

The house looks *small*.
noun   linking predicate
described   verb   adjective

2. An **ATTRIBUTIVE ADJECTIVE** is connected directly to the noun it describes and always precedes it.

The *good* children were praised.
attributive   noun
adjective   described

The family lives in a *small* house.
attributive   noun
adjective   described

IN SPANISH

As in English, descriptive adjectives can be identified as predicate or attribute adjectives according to the way they are connected to the noun they describe.

Spanish descriptive adjectives differ in two important ways from English descriptive adjectives.

1. While English descriptive adjectives never change form, all Spanish descriptive adjectives, predicate and attributive, change form in order to agree in gender and number with the noun or pronoun they modify.

   Most adjectives change the final "**-o**" of the masculine singular form to "**-a**" to make the feminine form and add "**-s**" to the masculine singular or the feminine singular form to make it plural.

*the **red** car*	el coche **rojo**
	masc. masc.
	sing. sing.
*the **red** table*	la mesa **roja**
	fem. fem. (final -o → -a)
	sing. sing.
*the **red** cars*	los coches **rojos**
	masc. masc. (**rojo** + -s)
	pl. pl.
*the **red** tables*	las mesas **rojas**
	fem. fem. (**roja** + -s)
	pl. pl.

2. While English descriptive adjectives always come before the noun they modify, most, but not all, Spanish descriptive adjectives come after the noun they modify.

   Ella lee un libro **interesante**.
   *She is reading an **interesting** book.*

   However, some common Spanish descriptive adjectives come before the noun they modify.

   Juan es un **buen** chico.
   *John is a **good** boy.*

Your textbook will tell you, and you will have to learn, which Spanish descriptive adjectives precede and which follow the noun they modify.

80 **NOUNS USED AS ADJECTIVES**

Occasionally, a noun is used as an adjective; that is, it is used to modify another noun.

IN ENGLISH

When a noun is used to describe another noun, the structure is as follows: the describing noun (adjective) + the noun described.

<table>
<tr><td>Spanish is easy.</td><td>The Spanish class is crowded.</td></tr>
<tr><td>|</td><td>| |</td></tr>
<tr><td>noun</td><td>adjective noun described</td></tr>
</table>

90

<table>
<tr><td>Chemistry is difficult.</td><td>The chemistry books are expensive.</td></tr>
<tr><td>|</td><td>| |</td></tr>
<tr><td>noun</td><td>adjective noun described</td></tr>
</table>

IN SPANISH

It is important that you recognize a noun acting as an adjective because it remains a noun and does not change form. In the examples below, you will see that the noun described and the noun acting as an adjective have different genders and numbers.

100 When a noun is used as an adjective, the structure is as follows: the noun described + **de** *(of)* + the describing noun (adjective) without an article.

<table>
<tr><td>the Spanish class</td><td>=</td><td>la clase de español</td></tr>
<tr><td>| |</td><td></td><td>| |</td></tr>
<tr><td>el español la clase</td><td></td><td>fem. sing. masc. sing.</td></tr>
<tr><td></td><td></td><td>noun   noun/adjective</td></tr>
<tr><td></td><td></td><td>described</td></tr>
</table>

<table>
<tr><td>the chemistry books</td><td>=</td><td>los libros de química</td></tr>
<tr><td>| |</td><td></td><td>| |</td></tr>
<tr><td>la química los libros</td><td></td><td>masc. pl. fem. sing.</td></tr>
<tr><td></td><td></td><td>noun   noun/adjective</td></tr>
<tr><td></td><td></td><td>described</td></tr>
</table>

✎ **REVIEW**

Circle the adjectives in the sentences below.
- Draw an arrow from the adjective you circled to the noun or pronoun described.

1. The young man was reading a Spanish newspaper.

2. She looked pretty in her new red dress.

3. It is interesting.

4. The old piano could still produce good music.

5. Paul was tired after his long walk.

Flashcards (see *Tips for learning Vocabulary,* pp. 1-3)

1. Create flashcards indicating the adjective twice on the Spanish side, once modifying a masculine noun and once modifying a feminine noun. This will show you the masculine and feminine forms of the adjective.

un coche **rojo**	*a **red** car*
una mesa **roja**	*a **red** table*

2. If the adjective has irregular singular or plural forms, illustrate them.

el hombre **español**	*the **Spanish** man*
los hombres **españoles**	*the **Spanish** men*
la mujer **española**	*the **Spanish** woman*
las mujeres **españolas**	*the **Spanish** women*

Practice

Write short sentences in Spanish using the descriptive adjectives you have learned, concentrating on the agreement of the adjectives with the nouns they modify.

CHAPTER

WHAT IS MEANT BY COMPARISON OF ADJECTIVES?

The term **COMPARISON OF ADJECTIVES** is used when two or more persons or things have the same quality (height, size, color, any characteristic) indicated by a descriptive adjective and we want to show which of these persons or things has a greater, lesser, or equal degree of that quality.

comparison of adjectives

Paul is *tall* but Mary is *taller*.

adjective   adjective
modifies *Paul*   modifies *Mary*

Both nouns, Paul and Mary, have the same quality indicated by the adjective *tall,* and we want to show that Mary has a greater degree of that quality (i.e., she is *taller* than Paul).

In English and in Spanish there are two types of comparison: comparative and superlative.

COMPARATIVE

The comparative compares a quality of a person or thing with the same quality in another person or thing. The comparison can indicate that one or the other has more, less, or the same amount of that quality.

IN ENGLISH

Let's go over the three degrees of comparison:

1. The comparison of **GREATER DEGREE** (more) is formed differently depending on the length of the adjective being compared.

   - short adjective + *-er* + ***than***

     Paul is tall*er than* Mary.
     Susan is old*er than* her sister.

   - ***more*** + longer adjective + ***than***

     Mary is *more* intelligent *than* John.
     His car is *more* expensive *than* ours.

2. The comparison of **LESSER DEGREE** (less) is formed as follows: ***not as*** + adjective + ***as***, or ***less*** + adjective + ***than***.

Mary is *not as* tall *as* Paul.
My car is *less* expensive *than* your car.

3. The comparison of **EQUAL DEGREE** (same) is formed as follows: *as* + adjective + *as*.

Robert is *as* tall *as* Mary.
My car is *as* expensive *as* his car.

IN SPANISH

As in English, the comparative has the same three degrees of comparison of adjectives.

Like all Spanish adjectives, Spanish comparative adjectives agree with the noun they modify. Although comparative adjectives refer to more than one noun or pronoun, they agree with the first noun or pronoun mentioned.

1. The comparison of **GREATER DEGREE** is formed as follows: **más** *(more)* + adjective + **que** *(than)*.

María es **más alta que** Juan.
          |
          agrees with first noun mentioned → María
*Mary is **taller than** John.*

2. The comparison of **LESSER DEGREE** is formed as follows: **menos** *(less)* + adjective + **que** *(than)*.

Juan es **menos alto que** María.
          |
          agrees with first noun mentioned → Juan
*John is **less tall than** Mary.*

3. The comparison of **EQUAL DEGREE** is formed as follows: **tan** *(as)* + adjective + **como** *(as)*.

María es **tan alta como** Roberto.
          |
          agrees with first noun mentioned → María
*María is **as tall as** Robert.*

SUPERLATIVE

The superlative is used to stress the highest or lowest degrees of a quality.

IN ENGLISH

Let's go over the two degrees of the superlative:

1. The superlative of **GREATEST DEGREE** is formed differently depending on the length of the adjective.

   ▪ *the* + short adjective + *-est*

Mary is *the* smart*est*.
My car is *the* cheap*est* on the market.

- ▪ *the most* + long adjective

Mary is *the most* intelligent.
His car is *the most* expensive.

2. The superlative of LOWEST DEGREE is formed as follows: *the least* + adjective.

Paul is *the least* active.
Her car is *the least* expensive of all.

IN SPANISH

There are the same two degrees of the superlative:

1. The superlative of GREATEST DEGREE is formed as follows: **el, la, los** or **las** (depending on the gender and number of the noun described) + **más** *(most)* + adjective.

Juan es **el más bajo** de la familia.
    masc. sing.
*John is **the shortest** in the family.*

María es **la más alta**.
    fem. sing.
*Mary is **the tallest**.*

Carlos y Roberto son **los más divertidos** de la clase.
    masc. pl.
*Charles and Robert are **the funniest** in the class.*

Teresa y Gloria son **las más inteligentes**.
    fem. pl.
*Teresa and Gloria are **the most intelligent**.*

2. The superlative of LOWEST DEGREE is formed as follows: **el, la, los** or **las** (depending on the gender and number of the noun described) + **menos** *(least)* + adjective.

Mi coche es **el menos caro**.
    masc. sing.
*My car is **the least expensive**.*

CAREFUL — In English and in Spanish, a few adjectives have irregular forms of comparison which you will have to memorize individually.

ADJECTIVE	Esta manzana es **buena.**
	*This apple is **good.***
COMPARATIVE	Esta manzana es **mejor.**
	*This apple is **better.***
SUPERLATIVE	Esta manzana es **la mejor.**
	*This apple is **the best.***

120

✎ REVIEW

Underline the comparative and superlative adjectives in the sentences below.

- Draw an arrow from the adjective to the noun or pronoun it modifies.
- Circle the various degrees of comparison: superlative (S), comparative of greater degree (C+), comparative of equal degree (C=), or comparative of lesser degree (C-).

1. The teacher is older than the students.   S   C+   C=   C-

2. He is less intelligent than I am.   S   C+   C=   C-

3. Mary is as tall as Paul.   S   C+   C=   C-

4. That boy is the worst in the school.   S   C+   C=   C-

5. Paul is a better student than Mary.   S   C+   C=   C-

WHAT IS A POSSESSIVE ADJECTIVE?

1   A **POSSESSIVE ADJECTIVE** is a word that describes a noun
by showing who possesses that noun.

> Whose house is that? It's *my* house.
>> *My* shows who possesses the noun *house*. The
>> possessor is "me." The object possessed is *house*.

IN ENGLISH

Like subject pronouns, possessive adjectives are identified
according to the person they represent (see p. 33).

10

     SINGULAR POSSESSOR

1ˢᵗ PERSON		my
2ⁿᵈ PERSON		your
	MASCULINE	his
3ᴿᴰ PERSON	FEMININE	her
	NEUTER	its

     PLURAL POSSESSOR

1ˢᵗ PERSON	our
2ⁿᵈ PERSON	your
3ᴿᴰ PERSON	their

20   A possessive adjective changes to identify the possessor,
regardless of the objects possessed.

> Is that John's house? Yes, it is *his* house.
> Is that Mary's house? Yes, it is *her* house.
>> Although the object possessed is the same *(house)*, different
>> possessive adjectives *(his* and *her)* are used because the pos-
>> sessors are different *(John* and *Mary)*.

> Is that John's house? Yes, it is *his* house.
> Are those John's keys? Yes, they are *his* keys.
>> Although the objects possessed are different *(house* and
30 >> *keys)*, the same possessive adjective *(his)* is used because the
>> possessor is the same *(John)*.

IN SPANISH

Like English, a Spanish possessive adjective changes to
identify the possessor, but unlike English it also agrees,
like all Spanish adjectives, in gender and number with the
noun possessed.

For example, in the phrase **nuestro hermano** *(our brother)* the possessor *(our)* is indicated by the first letters of the 1st person plural possessive adjective **nuestr-**, and the gender and number of the noun possessed, **hermano** *(brother)*, which is masculine singular, is reflected in the masculine singular ending **-o**. Let us see what happens when we change *our brother* to *our sister*.

> *We love **our sister.***
> Queremos a **nuestra hermana**.
> $\qquad$ fem. sing. ending
> 1st pers. pl.
> possessor

> The first letters **nuestr-** remain the same because the possessor is still the 1st person plural, but the ending changes to **-a** to agree with **hermana** *(sister)* which is feminine singular.

Spanish has two sets of possessive adjectives: the STRESSED POSSESSIVE ADJECTIVES and the UNSTRESSED POSSESSIVE ADJECTIVES. The short, unstressed forms are the most common and will be considered first.

SPANISH UNSTRESSED POSSESSIVE ADJECTIVES

My, your (tú, usted, ustedes **forms**), **his, her, their**
In Spanish, each of the above possessive adjectives has two forms, a singular and a plural form. You will choose the one that agrees with the number of the noun possessed.

To choose the correct form of the possessive adjective:

1. Indicate the possessor. This is shown by the first two letters of the possessive adjective.

my	**mi**
your [tú form]	**tu**
his	
her	
your [usted form]	**su**
their	
your [ustedes form]	

2. Choose the ending according to the number of the noun possessed.
   - noun possessed is singular → the form of the possessive adjective does not change

     Ana lee **mi** libro. $\qquad$ *Ana reads **my** book.*
     $\quad$ noun possessed singular
     Ana lee **tu** libro. $\qquad$ *Ana reads **your** book.*
     Ana lee **su** libro. $\qquad$ *Ana reads **her** (**his, your, their**) book.*

- noun possessed is plural → add -s to the possessive adjective

Ana lee **mis** libros.   *Ana reads **my** books.*
       |
    noun possessed plural
Ana lee **tus** libros.   *Ana reads **your** books.*
Ana lee **sus** libros.   *Ana reads **her (his, your, their)** books.*

Because the possessive adjective **su** has many meanings, Spanish speakers often replace it with the phrase: noun + **de** + pronoun.

	el libro **de él**	*his book*
	el libro **de ella**	*her book*
	el libro **de Ud.**	*your book*
su libro	el libro **de ellos**	*their book*
	el libro **de ellas**	*their book*
	el libro **de Uds.**	*your book*

You will have to rely on context to establish the English equivalent of the possessive adjectives **su** and **sus**.

Let us apply the above steps to examples:

*I am looking for **my** car.*
    1. POSSESSOR: *my* → 1ˢᵗ pers. sing. → **mi**
    2. NUMBER NOUN POSSESSED: **coche** *(car)* → singular
    3. SELECTION: **mi**
Busco **mi** coche.

*I am looking for **my** keys.*
    1. POSSESSOR: *my* → 1ˢᵗ pers. sing. → **mi**
    2. NUMBER NOUN POSSESSED: **llaves** *(keys)* → plural
    3. SELECTION: **mi- + -s**
Busco **mis** llaves.

Our, your (vosotros **form**)

In Spanish, the two possessive adjectives above have four forms, a masculine singular, a feminine singular, a masculine plural, and a feminine plural. You will choose the one that agrees with the gender and number of the noun possessed.

To choose the correct form of the possessive adjective:

1. Indicate the possessor. This is shown by the first letters of the possessive adjective.

our   **nuestr-**
your [vosotros form]   **vuestr-**

2. Choose the ending according to the gender and number of the noun possessed.

- noun possessed is masculine singular → add **-o**

  Ana lee **nuestro** libro. *Ana reads **our** book.*
  |
  noun possessed masc. sing.

  Ana lee **vuestro** libro. *Ana reads **your** book.*

- noun possessed is feminine singular → add **-a**

  Ana lee **nuestra** revista. *Ana reads **our** magazine.*
  |
  noun possessed fem. sing.

  Ana lee **vuestra** revista. *Ana reads **your** magazine.*

- noun possessed is masculine plural → add **-os**

  Ana lee **nuestros** libros. *Ana reads **our** books.*
  |
  noun possessed masc. pl.

  Ana lee **vuestros** libros. *Ana reads **your** books.*

- noun possessed is feminine plural → add **-as**

  Ana lee **nuestras** revistas. *Ana reads **our** magazines.*
  |
  noun possessed fem. pl.

  Ana lee **vuestras** revistas. *Ana reads **your** magazines.*

Let us apply the above steps to examples:

*We are looking for **our** car.*
1. POSSESSOR: *our* → 1ˢᵗ pers. pl. → **nuestr-**
2. GENDER & NUMBER NOUN POSSESSED: **coche** *(car)* → masc. sing.
3. SELECTION: **nuestr- + -o**
Buscamos **nuestro** coche.

*We are looking for **our** keys.*
1. POSSESSOR: *our* → 1ˢᵗ pers. pl. → **nuestr-**
2. GENDER & NUMBER NOUN POSSESSED: **llaves** *(keys)* → fem. pl.
3. SELECTION: **nuestr- + -as**
Buscamos **nuestras** llaves.

Notice that unstressed possessive adjectives are placed before the noun they modify.

CAREFUL — Make sure that the ending of possessive adjectives agrees with the noun modified and not with the possessor.

SPANISH STRESSED POSSESSIVE ADJECTIVES
Spanish also has another set of possessive adjectives called STRESSED POSSESSIVE ADJECTIVES. They are used to add emphasis to the possessor and correspond to the English "of mine," "of yours," etc.

Where is that *dress of mine?*

instead of *my dress*

Where are those *books of yours?*

instead of *your books*

The use of these stressed forms is more common in Spanish than in English.

The stressed possessive adjectives have four forms, a masculine singular, a feminine singular, a masculine plural, and a feminine plural. You will choose the one that agrees with the gender and number of the noun possessed.

To choose the correct stressed possessive adjective:

1. Indicate the possessor. This is shown by the first letters of the possessive adjective.

mine, of mine	**mí-**
your, of yours [**tú** form]	**tuy-**
his, of his	
her, of hers	**suy-**
your, of yours [**usted** form]	
our, of ours	**nuestr-**
your, of yours [**vosotros** form]	**vuestr-**
their, of theirs	
your, of yours [**ustedes** form]	**suy-**

2. Choose the ending according to the gender and number of the noun possessed.
   - noun possessed is masculine singular → add **-o**

     Ana lee un libro **mío**.

     noun possessed masc. sing.

     Ana is reading a book of mine.

   - noun possessed is feminine singular→ add **-a**

     Ana lee una revista **mía**.

     noun possessed fem. sing.

     Ana is reading a magazine of mine.

   - noun possessed is masculine plural → add **-os**

     Ana lee unos libros **míos**.

     noun possessed masc. pl.

     Ana is reading some books of mine.

- noun possessed is feminine plural → add -as

    Ana lee unas revistas **mías**.

    |
    noun possessed fem. pl.

    Ana is reading some magazines of mine.

Let us apply the above steps to examples:

> *This car is John's. My car is in the garage.*   210
> 1. POSSESSOR: *my* → 1st pers. sing. → **mí-**
> 2. GENDER & NUMBER NOUN POSSESSED: **coche** (*car*) → masc. sing.
> 3. SELECTION: **mí- + -o**

El coche **mío** está en el garaje.

> *These chairs of yours are very comfortable.*
> 1. POSSESSOR: *of yours* → 2nd pers. sing. → **tuy-**
> 2. GENDER & NUMBER NOUN POSSESSED: **sillas** (*chairs*) → fem. pl.
> 3. SELECTION: **tuy- + -as**

Estas sillas **tuyas** son muy cómodas.   220

Notice that stressed possessive adjectives are placed after the noun they modify.

SUMMARY

Here are two charts you can use as a reference.

POSSESSOR		UNSTRESSED POSSESSIVE ADJECTIVES	
		NOUN POSSESSED	
		SINGULAR	PLURAL
my	MASC. FEM.	mi	mis
your [tú form]	MASC. FEM.	tu	tus
his, her, *your* [usted form]	MASC. FEM.	su	sus
our	MASC. FEM.	nuestro nuestra	nuestros nuestras
your [vosotros form]	MASC. FEM.	vuestro vuestra	vuestros vuestras
their, *your* [ustedes form]	MASC. FEM.	su	sus

230

240

		STRESSED POSSESSIVE ADJECTIVES	
POSSESSOR		**NOUN POSSESSED**	
		SINGULAR	PLURAL
my, of mine	MASC.	mío	míos
	FEM.	mía	mías
your [tú form]	MASC.	tuyo	tuyos
	FEM.	tuya	tuyas
his, her, *your* [usted form]	MASC.	suyo	suyos
	FEM.	suya	suyas
our	MASC.	nuestro	nuestros
	FEM.	nuestra	nuestras
your [vosotros form]	MASC.	vuestro	vuestros
	FEM.	vuestra	vuestras
their, *your* [ustedes form]	MASC.	suyo	suyos
	FEM.	suya	suyas

✎ REVIEW

Circle the possessive adjectives in the sentences below.
- Draw an arrow from the possessive adjective to the noun it modifies.
- Circle singular (S) or plural (P) to indicate the ending of the Spanish possessive adjective.
- Using the charts in this section, fill in the Spanish unstressed possessive adjective in the Spanish sentences below.

1. I put my book on the desk.

      NOUN MODIFIED IN SPANISH: masculine   S   P

Puse _____ libro sobre el escritorio.

2. Mary is wearing your [familiar] boots.

      NOUN MODIFIED IN SPANISH: feminine   S   P

María lleva_____ botas.

3. Roberto is looking for his mother.

      NOUN MODIFIED IN SPANISH: feminine   S   P

Roberto busca a _____ madre.

4. Our children are very young.

      NOUN MODIFIED IN SPANISH: masculine   S   P

_____ hijos son muy jóvenes.

Pattern (see *Tips for Learning Word Forms,* pp. 3-4)

Flashcards

1. Create one card for each of the persons (1st, 2nd, and 3rd sing. and pl.) with an example of the different forms of the unstressed possessive adjectives.

mi coche, **mis** coches	*my car, my cars*
mi casa, **mis** casas	*my house, my houses*
tu coche, **tus** coches	*your car, your cars*
tu casa, **tus** casas	*your house, your houses*
nuestro coche, **nuestros** coches	*our car, our cars*
nuestra casa, **nuestras** casas	*our house, our houses*

2. On the card for the 3rd person, to reinforce the fact that *his, her, your,* and *their* can be either **su** or **sus** and that possessive adjectives agree with the thing possessed and not with the possessor, write short Spanish sentences with 3rd person possessive adjectives modifying masculine and feminine nouns in the singular and plural.

Juan vende **su libro.**	*John sells **his (her, your, their) book.***
Ana vende **su libro.**	*Ana sells **his (her, your, their) book.***
Juan vende **su casa.**	*John sells **his (her, your, their) house.***
Ana vende **su casa.**	*Ana sells **his (her, your, their) house.***
Juan vende **sus libros.**	*John sells **his (her, your, their) books.***
Ana vende **sus libros.**	*Ana sells **his (her, your, their) books.***
Juan vende **sus casas.**	*John sells **his (her, your, their) houses.***
Ana vende **sus casas.**	*Ana sells **his (her, your, their) houses.***

3. Repeat steps No. 1 and 2 above with the stressed possessive adjectives.

Practice

1. Sort out your noun flashcards and select a few masculine and feminine nouns.

   ■ Look at the Spanish side and go through the cards writing down (on a separate piece of paper) or saying out loud the noun preceded by the correct forms of the unstressed possessive adjectives.

el cuarto	*room*
mi cuarto, tu cuarto, su cuarto, nuestro cuarto, vuestro cuarto	
la casa	*house*
mi casa, tu casa, su casa, nuestra casa, vuestra casa	
los libros	*books*
mis libros, tus libros, sus libros, nuestros libros, vuestros libros	

   ■ Look at the Spanish side and go through the cards writing down or saying out loud the noun with the correct forms of the stressed possessive adjectives.

el cuarto	*room*
el cuarto mío, el cuarto tuyo, el cuarto suyo, el cuarto nuestro, el cuarto vuestro	

2. Use these noun cards to practice the forms for the 3rd pers. sing. and pl. (*his, her, your, their*) going from English to Spanish.

*his room, **her** room, **your** room, **their** room*	**su** cuarto

CHAPTER

33

WHAT IS AN INTERROGATIVE ADJECTIVE?

An **INTERROGATIVE ADJECTIVE** is a word that asks for
information about a noun.

Which book do you want?
|
asks information about the noun *book*

IN ENGLISH
The words **which** and **what** are called interrogative adjectives when they come in front of a noun and are used to ask a question about that noun.

Which instructor is teaching the course?
What courses are you taking?

IN SPANISH
There are two interrogative adjectives: 1. **qué** which corresponds to the English *which* or *what* and 2. the forms of **cuánto** meaning *how much* or *how many*.[1]

1. *which* or *what* + noun → **qué** + noun

   Qué is invariable; that is, it does not change form.

   ¿**Qué** revista lees?
   What magazine are you reading?

   ¿**Qué** libros quieres?
   Which books do you want?

2. *how much* or *how many* + noun → **cuánto** + noun

   Cuánto changes forms to agree in number and gender with the noun it modifies. Therefore, in order to choose the correct form of **cuánto**, begin by analyzing the noun modified.

   - noun modified is masculine singular → **cuánto**

     ¿**Cuánto** dinero necesitas?
     Dinero *(money)* is masculine singular, so the word for "how much" must be masculine singular.
     How much money do you need?

---

[1]**Qué** is used in standard Spanish. In certain areas of the Spanish-speaking world **cuál** and **cuáles** can function as interrogative adjectives: ¿**Cuál** libro quieres? *Which book do you want?*

- noun modified is feminine singular → **cuánta**

  ¿Cuánta sopa quieres?

  Sopa *(soup)* is feminine singular, so the word for "how much" must be feminine singular.

  How much soup do you want?

- noun modified is masculine plural → **cuántos**

  ¿Cuántos discos tienes?

  Discos *(CDs)* is masculine plural, so the word for "how many" must be masculine plural.

  How many CDs do you have?

- noun modified is feminine plural → **cuántas**

  ¿Cuántas maletas traes?

  Maletas *(suitcases)* is feminine plural, so the word for "how many" must be feminine plural.

  How many suitcases are you bringing?

CAREFUL — The word *what* is not always an interrogative adjective. It can also be an interrogative pronoun (see *What is an Interrogative Pronoun?*, p. 172). When it is a pronoun, *what* (**qué**) is not followed by a noun.

What *is on the table?*
|
interrogative pronoun

¿Qué hay en la mesa?

The expression "how many" is not always an interrogative adjective. It can also be an interrogative pronoun. When it is a pronoun, *how many* (**cuánto**) is not followed by a noun.

How many *do you need?*
|_____|
interrogative pronoun

¿Cuántos necesitas?

It is important that you distinguish interrogative adjectives from interrogative pronouns because, in Spanish, sometimes different words are used and they follow different rules.

✎ **REVIEW**

A. Circle the interrogative adjectives in the sentences below.
- Draw an arrow from the interrogative adjective to the noun it modifies.

1. Which book is yours?

2. Please tell me what exercises are due tomorrow.

3. Which house do you live in?

B. Circle the interrogative adjectives in the sentences below.
- Draw an arrow from the interrogative adjective to the noun it modifies.
- Indicate if the noun modified is singular (S) or plural (P).
- Fill in the Spanish interrogative adjective in the Spanish sentences below.

1. How many shirts did you buy?

　　　NOUN MODIFIED IN SPANISH: feminine　　　S　　　P

　　¿ _____ camisas compraste?

2. How much wine are you bringing to the party?

　　　NOUN MODIFIED IN SPANISH: masculine　　　S　　　P

　　¿ _____ vino traes a la fiesta?

3. How many telephones are there in your house?

　　　NOUN MODIFIED IN SPANISH: masculine　　　S　　　P

　　¿ _____ teléfonos hay en tu casa?

4. How much salad do you want?

　　　NOUN MODIFIED IN SPANISH: feminine　　　S　　　P

　　¿ _____ ensalada quieres?

WHAT IS A DEMONSTRATIVE ADJECTIVE?

1

A **DEMONSTRATIVE ADJECTIVE** is a word used
to point out a noun.

This book is interesting.
|
points out the noun *book*

IN ENGLISH

The demonstrative adjectives are **this** and **that** in the singular and **these** and **those** in the plural. They are rare examples of English adjectives agreeing in number with the noun they modify: *this* changes to *these* and *that* changes to *those* when they modify a plural noun.

10

SINGULAR	PLURAL
this cat	*these* cats
that man	*those* men

This and *these* refer to persons or objects near the speaker, and *that* and *those* refer to persons or objects away from the speaker.

IN SPANISH

There are three sets of demonstrative adjectives and they all agree in gender and number with the nouns they modify.

20

In order to say *"this* house" or *"that* room" start by determining where the person or object is in relation to the speaker or the person spoken to. Then, determine the gender and number of the noun you wish to point out and make the demonstrative adjective agree with that noun.

1. noun near the speaker *(this, these)* → a form of **este**
   - noun modified is masculine singular → **este**

      Este cuarto es grande.
         Cuarto *(room)* is masculine singular, so the word for
         "this" must be masculine singular.

30

      This room is large.

   - noun modified is feminine singular → **esta**

      Esta casa es grande.
         Casa *(house)* is feminine singular, so the word for
         "this" must be feminine singular.

      This house is large.

- noun modified is masculine plural → **estos**

  Estos cuartos son grandes.
  > **Cuartos** *(rooms)* is masculine plural, so the word for
  > "these" must be masculine plural.

  These rooms are large.

- noun modified is feminine plural → **estas**

  Estas casas son grandes.
  > **Casas** *(houses)* is feminine plural, so the word for
  > "these" must be feminine plural.

  These houses are large.

2. noun near the person spoken to *(that, those)* → a form of **ese**

- noun modified is masculine singular → **ese**

  Ese cuarto es grande.
  > **Cuarto** *(room)* is masculine singular, so the word for
  > "that" must be masculine singular.

  That room is large.

- noun modified is feminine singular → **esa**

  Esa casa es grande.
  > **Casa** *(house)* is feminine singular, so the word for
  > "that" must be feminine singular.

  That house is large.

- noun modified is masculine plural → **esos**

  Esos cuartos son grandes.
  > **Cuartos** *(rooms)* is masculine plural, so the word for
  > "those" must be masculine plural.

  Those rooms are large.

- noun modified is feminine plural → **esas**

  Esas casas son grandes.
  > **Casas** *(houses)* is feminine plural, so the word for
  > "those" must be feminine plural.

  Those houses are large.

3. noun away from both the speaker and the person spoken to *(that, those)* → a form of **aquel**

   Since English does not have this third set of demonstrative adjectives, there is no good translation for them.
Sometimes "over there" is added to imply the distance.

- noun modified is masculine singular → **aquel**

  Aquel cuarto es grande.
  > **Cuarto** *(room)* is masculine singular, so the word for
  > "that" must be masculine singular.

  That room (over there) is large.

- noun modified is feminine singular → **aquella**   80

    Aquella casa es grande.

    > Casa *(house)* is feminine singular, so the word for
    > "that" must be feminine singular.

    That house (over there) is large.

- noun modified is masculine plural → **aquellos**

    Aquellos cuartos son grandes.

    > Cuartos *(rooms)* is masculine plural, so the word for
    > "those" must be masculine plural.

    Those rooms (over there) are large.

- noun modified is feminine plural → **aquellas**   90

    Aquellas casas son grandes.

    > Casas *(houses)* is feminine plural, so the word for
    > "those" must be feminine plural.

    Those houses (over there) are large.

CAREFUL — These three sets of demonstrative adjectives may also function as demonstrative pronouns (see *What is a Demonstrative Pronoun?*, p. 180). As demonstrative pronouns they are not followed by a noun.

✎ **REVIEW**

Circle the demonstrative adjectives in the sentences below.
- Draw an arrow from the demonstrative adjective to the noun it modifies.
- Circle if the noun modified is singular (S) or plural (P).
- Fill in the Spanish demonstrative adjective in the Spanish sentences below.

1. They prefer that restaurant.

    NOUN MODIFIED IN SPANISH: masculine   S   P

    Prefieren _____ restaurante.

2. Those houses over there are very expensive.

    NOUN MODIFIED IN SPANISH: feminine   S   P

    _____ casas son muy caras.

3. I bought these shoes in Spain.

    NOUN MODIFIED IN SPANISH: masculine   S   P

    Compré _____ zapatos en España.

4. Do you want this magazine?

    NOUN MODIFIED IN SPANISH: feminine   S   P

    ¿Quieres _____ revista?

WHAT IS AN ADVERB?

An **ADVERB** is a word that describes a verb, an adjective,
or another adverb. It indicates
manner, degree, time, place.[1]

Mary drives *well*.
| |
verb adverb

The house is *very* big.
| |
adverb adjective

The girl ran *too quickly*.
| |
adverb adverb

IN ENGLISH

There are different types of adverbs:

- an **ADVERB OF MANNER** answers the question *how?* Adverbs
  of manner are the most common and they are easy to
  recognize because they end with *-ly*.

  Mary sings *beautifully*.
  Beautifully describes the verb *sings*; it tells you how Mary sings.

- an **ADVERB OF DEGREE** answers the question *how much?*
  Paul did *well* on the exam.

- an **ADVERB OF TIME** answers the question *when?*
  He will come *soon*.

- an **ADVERB OF PLACE** answers the question *where?*
  The children were left *behind*.

IN SPANISH

Most adverbs of manner can be recognized by the ending
-mente which corresponds to the English ending *-ly*.

fácil**mente**	*easily*
natural**mente**	*naturally*
rápida**mente**	*rapidly*

---

[1]In English and in Spanish, the structure for comparing adverbs is the same as the
structure for comparing adjectives (see *What is Meant by Comparison of Adjectives?*,
p. 114).

You will have to memorize adverbs as vocabulary items. The most important fact for you to remember is that adverbs are INVARIABLE; ie., they never change form.

CAREFUL — Remember that in English *good* is an adjective since it modifies a noun and *well* is an adverb since it modifies a verb.

> The student writes *good* English.
> > *Good* modifies the noun *English;* it is an adjective.

> The student writes *well*.
> > *Well* modifies the verb *writes;* it is an adverb.

Likewise, in Spanish **bueno** is an adjective meaning *good;* **bien** is the adverb meaning *well*.

> *The **good** students speak Spanish **well**.*
> > adjective   adverb
> Los estudiantes **buenos** hablan español **bien**.
> > masc. pl. adj.   adverb

✎ REVIEW

Circle the adverbs in the sentences below.
- Draw an arrow from the adverb to the word it modifies.

1. The students arrived early.

2. Paul learned the lesson really quickly.

3. The students were too tired to study.

4. He has a reasonably secure income.

5. Mary is a good student who speaks Spanish very well.

STUDY TIPS — ADVERBS

Flashcards (see *Tips for Learning Vocabulary,* pp. 1-3)
1. Create flashcards for each Spanish adverb that you learn; indicate its English equivalent.
> siempre   *always*
> rápidamente   *rapidly, quickly*
2. Add sample sentences illustrating the adverb within a sentence.
> Manuel viene a clase **siempre**.   *Manuel **always** comes to class.*
> Ana maneja **rápidamente**.   *Ana drives **fast** (rapidly).*

CHAPTER

36

WHAT IS A CONJUNCTION?

¹

A **CONJUNCTION** is a word that links two
or more words or groups of words.

He had to choose between good *and* evil.

|

conjunction

They left *because* they were bored.

|

conjunction

IN ENGLISH

There are two kinds of conjunctions: coordinating and
subordinating.

- a **COORDINATING CONJUNCTION** joins words, phrases (groups
of words without a verb), and clauses (groups of words
with a verb) that are equal; it *coordinates* elements of
equal rank. The major coordinating conjunctions are
and, but, or, nor, for, and *yet.*

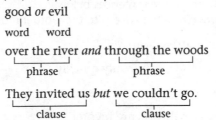

In the last example, each of the two clauses, "they
invited us" and "we couldn't go," expresses a complete
thought; therefore, each clause could stand alone.
When a clause expresses a complete thought and can
stand alone, it is called a **MAIN CLAUSE**. In the above sentence, the coordinating conjunction *but* links two main
clauses.

- a **SUBORDINATING CONJUNCTION** joins a main clause to
a dependent clause; it *subordinates* one clause to another. A **DEPENDENT CLAUSE** does not express a complete
thought; therefore, it cannot stand alone. There are various types of dependent clauses. A clause introduced by
a subordinating conjunction is called a **SUBORDINATE**

CLAUSE. Typical subordinating conjunctions are *before, after, since, although, because, if, unless, so that, while, that,* and *when.*

₄₀

```
      subordinate clause        main clause
    ┌──────────┴──────────┐   ┌──────┴──────┐
    Although we were invited, we didn't go.
        │
    subordinating
    conjunction
```

```
    main clause     subordinate clause
    ┌────┴────┐   ┌──────────┴──────────┐
    They left because they were bored.
                    │
              subordinating
              conjunction
```

₅₀

```
    main clause subordinate clause
    ┌───┴───┐  ┌──────┴──────┐
    He said that he was tired.
                 │
            subordinating
            conjunction
```

In the above examples, "although we were invited," "because they were bored," and "that he was tired," are all subordinate clauses. They are not complete thoughts and each is introduced by a subordinating conjunction.

Notice that the subordinate clause may come either at the beginning of the sentence or after the main clause.

₆₀

IN SPANISH

Conjunctions must be memorized as vocabulary items. Just as adverbs and prepositions, conjunctions are INVARIABLE; i.e., they never change their form.

✎ REVIEW

Circle the coordinating and subordinating conjunctions in the sentences below.
- Underline the words each conjunction serves to coordinate or to subordinate.

1. Mary and Paul were going to study French or Spanish.

2. She did not study because she was too tired.

3. Not only had he forgotten his ticket, but he had forgotten

   his passport as well.

Flashcards (see *Tips for Learning Vocabulary,* pp. 1-3)

1. Create flashcards indicating Spanish conjunctions and their English equivalent.

pero	*but*
porque	*because*
y	*and*

2. When you learn the subjunctive (see *What is the Subjunctive,* p. 81), on the conjunction cards indicate the ones that are followed by the subjunctive instead of the indicative. Add an example as a reinforcement.

para que (+ subj.)	*in order to, so that*
Mi madre trabaja **para que**	*My mother works **so that***
yo pueda ir a la universidad.	*I can go to the university.*

Practice

Write a series of sentences using various conjunctions. Make sure to put the verb that follows the conjunction in the subjunctive, if the conjunction requires it.

WHAT IS A PREPOSITION?

A **PREPOSITION** is a word that shows the relationship of
one word (usually a noun or pronoun) to another word
(usually another noun or pronoun) in the sentence.

prepositional phrase

Paul has an appointment *after* school.

preposition   object of preposition

The noun or pronoun following the preposition is called the
OBJECT OF THE PREPOSITION. The preposition plus its object is
called a **PREPOSITIONAL PHRASE**.

IN ENGLISH

Prepositions normally indicate location, direction, or time.

- prepositions showing location or direction

    Paul was *in* the car.
    Mary put the books *on* the table.
    The students came directly *from* class.
    Mary went *to* school.

- prepositions showing time and date

    Many Spanish people go on vacation *in* August.
    On Mondays, they go to the university.
    I'm meeting him *at* 4:30 today.
    We're studying *before* the exam.
    Most people work *from* nine *to* five.

Other frequently used prepositions are: *during, since, with,
between, of, about.* Some prepositions are made up of more
than a single word: *because of, in front of, instead of, due to,
in spite of, on account of.*

IN SPANISH

You will have to memorize prepositions as vocabulary,
paying special attention to their meaning and use.
Prepositions are **INVARIABLE**, that is, they never change
form.

CAREFUL — Prepositions are tricky. Every language uses
prepositions differently. Do not assume that the same prepo-

sition is used in Spanish as in English, or even that a preposition will be needed in Spanish when you must use one in English and vice versa.

ENGLISH	SPANISH
CHANGE OF PREPOSITION	
to laugh *at*	reirse **de** *(of)*
to consist *of*	consistir **en** *(in)*
PREPOSITION	**NO PREPOSITION**
to look *for*	buscar
to look *at*	mirar
NO PREPOSITION	**PREPOSITION**
to leave	salir **de**
to enter	entrar **en**

A dictionary will usually give you the verb and the preposition which follows it, when one is required.

Do not translate an English verb + preposition with a word-for-word Spanish equivalent (see pp. 26-7).

 REVIEW

Circle the prepositions in the following sentences.

1. I will call you toward the end of the week.

2. His family returned from Peru last year.

3. The teacher walked around the room as she talked.

4. These days many men and women work at home.

5. The garden between the two houses was very small.

STUDY TIPS — PREPOSITIONS

Flashcards (see *Tips for Learning Vocabulary,* pp. 1-3)

Be careful when creating flashcards for prepositions because one English preposition can have several Spanish equivalents and vice versa. Always learn a preposition in a short sentence illustrating its usage.

1. Prepositions indicating the position of one object or person in relation to another are the easiest to learn because there is usually only one Spanish equivalent.

sobre	*on top of*
El libro está **sobre** la mesa.	*The book is **on top of** the table.*

detrás de	*behind*
Juan está **detrás de** María.	*John is **behind** Mary.*

2. Prepositions such as **a, de, en** have many English equivalents because their meaning varies according to the noun that follows. Indicate their varied meanings on the English side of the card.

a (+ location)	*to + location*
Voy **a** la universidad.	*I'm going **to** the university.*
a (+ time)	*at + time*
Salgo **a** las diez.	*I'm leaving **at** ten (o'clock).*
en (+ location)	*on + location, at + location*
El libro está **en** el escritorio.	*The book is **on** the desk.*
Juan está **en** el restaurante.	*John is **at** the restaurant.*

3. When you learn a verb that is usually followed by a particular preposition, indicate the preposition on the verb card and write a short sentence to illustrate its use.

entrar en	*to enter*
Entramos en la oficina	***We entered** the office*
a las ocho.	*at eight (o'clock).*

Practice

1. Following the examples under No. 1 above, think of two objects (or persons) and write Spanish sentences using prepositions placing the objects (or persons) in various positions in relation to one another.

Juan está **enfrente de** Carlos.	*Juan is **in front of** Carlos.*
Juan está **al lado de** Carlos.	*Juan is **next to** Carlos.*

2. Following the examples under No. 2 above, create short sentences using **a** + location, **en** + location, and **a** + time.

No voy **a** la fiesta.	*I'm not going **to** the party.*
Ricardo está **en** la biblioteca.	*Ricardo is **at** the library.*
La clase empieza **a** las nueve.	*The class begins **at** nine (o'clock).*

CHAPTER

38

WHAT ARE OBJECTS?

OBJECTS are nouns or pronouns indicating towards what or whom the action of the verb is directed.

Paul writes a *letter*.
    | |
  verb   object

He speaks to *Mary*.
    | |
  verb   object

The boy left with *his father*.
    | |
  verb   object

There are three types of objects: direct objects, indirect objects, and objects of a preposition. In this chapter we have limited the examples to noun objects. For examples with pronoun objects see *What are Direct and Indirect Object Pronouns?*, p. 147 and *What are Object of Preposition Pronouns?*, p. 156.

DIRECT OBJECT
IN ENGLISH

A direct object is a noun or pronoun that receives the action of the verb directly, without a preposition between the verb and the noun or pronoun. It answers the question *whom?* or *what?* asked after the verb.[1]

John sees *Mary*.
John sees *whom?* Mary.
Mary is the direct object.

John writes *a letter*.
John writes *what?* A letter.
A letter is the direct object.

Verbs can be classified as to whether or not they take a direct object.

- a **TRANSITIVE VERB** is a verb that takes a direct object. It is indicated by the abbreviation *v.t. (verbo transitivo)* in Spanish dictionaries.

---

[1]In this section, we will consider active sentences only (see *What is Meant by Active and Passive Voice?*, p. 104).

The boy *threw* the ball.
         | |
     transitive direct object

- an **INTRANSITIVE VERB** is a verb that does not require a direct object. It is indicated by the abbreviation *v.i. (verbo intransitivo)* in Spanish dictionaries.

Paul *is sleeping.*
        |
    intransitive

IN SPANISH

As in English, a direct object is a noun or pronoun that receives the action of the verb directly. It answers the question **¿quién?** *(whom?)* or **¿qué?** *(what?)* asked after the verb.

Juan escribe **una carta.**
    John writes *what?* A letter (**una carta**).
    Una carta is the direct object.
*John writes **a letter**.*

In Spanish a direct object noun referring to a person is preceded by the word "a." This is called the **PERSONAL a**. It does not have an English translation.

Juan ve **a María.**
     |
    personal **a** + direct object noun (person)
*John sees **Mary**.*

Juan ve **a las muchachas.**
     |
    personal **a** + direct object noun (persons)
*John sees **the girls**.*

Juan ve **al hombre.**
     |
    personal **a** + **el** + direct object noun (person)
*John sees **the man**.*

Juan ve **la casa.**
     |
    no personal **a** required, direct object noun (thing)
*John sees **the house**.*

INDIRECT OBJECT

IN ENGLISH

An indirect object is a noun or pronoun that receives the action of the verb indirectly. It answers the question *to whom?* or *to what?* asked after the verb.

John wrote *his brother.*
> He wrote *to whom?* His brother.
> *His brother* is the indirect object.

Sometimes the word *to* is included in the English sentence.[1]
> John spoke *to Paul and Mary.*
> John speaks *to whom?* To Paul and Mary.
> *Paul and Mary* are two indirect objects.

IN SPANISH

As in English, an indirect object is a noun or pronoun that receives the action of the verb indirectly with the preposition **a** *(to)* relating it to the verb. It answers the question **¿a quién?** *(to whom)* or **¿a qué?** *(to what?)* asked after the verb.

In Spanish, when an indirect object noun refers to a person an indirect object pronoun must be added before the verb. For instance, **le** is used when the indirect object noun is singular and **les** is used when the indirect object noun is plural (see *What are Direct and Indirect Object Pronouns?*, p. 147).

> Juan **le** escribió a su hermano.
> |
>   singular
> (word-for-word: *John (to him) wrote to his brother)*
> *John wrote (to) his brother.*

> Juan **les** habló a Pablo y a María.
> |
>   plural
> (word-for-word: *John (to them) spoke to Paul and Mary)*
> *John spoke (to) Paul and Mary.*

SENTENCES WITH A DIRECT AND AN INDIRECT OBJECT

A sentence may contain both a direct object and an indirect object which may be either nouns or pronouns. In this section we shall speak only of nouns as objects.

IN ENGLISH

When a sentence has both a direct and an indirect object, the following two word orders are possible:

1. subject (S) + verb (V) + indirect object (IO) + direct object (DO)

---

[1] In English "to Paul and Mary" is called a PREPOSITIONAL PHRASE because it is a phrase that begins with the preposition *to*; in this book we refer to noun and pronoun objects of the preposition *to* as indirect objects since that is how they function in Spanish.

John gave his sister a gift.
| | | |
S   V   IO   DO

> *Who* gave a gift? John.   120
> *John* is the subject.
>
> John gave *what?* A gift.
> *A gift* is the direct object.
>
> John gave a gift *to whom?* His sister.
> *His sister* is the indirect object.

2. subject + verb + direct object + *to* + indirect object

John gave a gift to his sister.
| | | |
S   V   DO   IO

The first structure, under 1, is the most common. How-   130
ever, because there is no *"to"* preceding the indirect
object, it is more difficult to identify its function than in
the second structure.

Regardless of the word order, the function of the words
in these two sentences is the same because they answer
the same question. Be sure to ask the questions to establish the function of words in a sentence.

IN SPANISH

Unlike English, when a sentence has both a direct and an   140
indirect object noun, there is only one word order possible (structure 2): subject + **le** or **les** + verb + direct object +
a *(to)* + indirect object.

Juan **le** dio **un regalo a su hermana.**
| | | | | |
S   **le**   V   DO   **a**   IO

(word-for-word: *John (to her) gave a gift to his sister*)

John gave his sister a gift.
John gave a gift to his sister.

OBJECT OF A PREPOSITION   150
IN ENGLISH

An object of a preposition is a noun or pronoun that follows a preposition and is related to it. It answers the question *whom?* or *what?* asked after the preposition.

> John is leaving *with Mary.*
>
> John is leaving *with whom?* With Mary.
> *Mary* is the object of the preposition *with.*
>
> The baby eats *with a spoon.*
>
> The baby eats *with what?* With a spoon.
> *A spoon* is the object of the preposition *with.*   160

IN SPANISH

As in English, an object of a preposition is a noun or pronoun that follows a preposition and is related to it. It answers the question **¿quién?** or **¿qué?** asked after the preposition.

> Pablo sale **con María**.
> *Paul is leaving **with Mary**.*

> Juan trabaja **para el Sr. Jones**.
> *John works **for Mr. Jones**.*

170

RELATIONSHIP OF A VERB TO ITS OBJECT

The relationship between a verb and its object is often different in English and Spanish. For example, a verb may take an object of a preposition in English but a direct object in Spanish. Therefore, when you learn a Spanish verb, it is important to find out if it is followed by a preposition, and if so, which one. Your textbook, as well as dictionaries, will indicate when a Spanish verb needs a preposition before an object.

180

Here are differences you are likely to encounter.

1. ENGLISH: object of a preposition → SPANISH: direct object

> *I am looking **for the book**.*
> FUNCTION IN ENGLISH: object of a preposition
> I am looking *for what?* The book.
> *The book* is the object of the preposition *for*.

> Busco **el libro**.
> FUNCTION IN SPANISH: direct object
> **¿Qué busco? El libro.**
> Since **buscar** *(to look for)* is not followed by a preposi-

190

> tion, it takes a direct object.

Many common verbs require an object of a preposition in English, but a direct object in Spanish.

*to look **for***	buscar
*to look **at***	mirar
*to ask **for***	pedir
*to listen **to***	escuchar
*to wait **for***	esperar
*to wait **on***	servir

2. ENGLISH: direct object → SPANISH: object of a preposition

200

> *John remembers **his apartment** in Madrid.*
> FUNCTION IN ENGLISH: direct object
> John remember *what?* His apartment.
> *His apartment* is the direct object.

Juan se acuerda **de su apartamento** en Madrid.
FUNCTION IN SPANISH: object of a preposition
¿De qué se acuerda Juan? De su apartamento.
(word-for-word: *Of what does John remember?*
Of his apartment.) The verb **acordarse** *(to remember)* is followed by the preposition **de** *(of);* it requires an object of
the preposition **de**.

A few common verbs require a direct object in English
but an object of a preposition in Spanish.

to enjoy	gozar **de**
to enter	entrar **en**
to forget	olvidarse **de**
to leave	salir **de**
to marry	casarse **con**
to play	jugar **a**
to remember	acordarse **de**

CAREFUL — Always identify the function of a word within
the language in which you are working; do not mix English
and Spanish patterns.

SUMMARY

Your ability to recognize the three types of objects is essen-
tial. A different Spanish pronoun is used for the English pronoun *him* depending on whether *him* is a direct object (**lo**),
an indirect object (**le**), or an object of a preposition (**él**).

The different types of objects in a sentence can be identified by establishing whether they answer a question which
requires a preposition or not and, if so, which one.

DIRECT OBJECT — An object that receives the action of the verb
directly.

INDIRECT OBJECT — An object that receives the action of the
verb indirectly, sometimes with the preposition *to.*

OBJECT OF A PREPOSITION — An object that follows a preposition and is related to it.

✎ REVIEW

Find the objects in the sentences below:
- Next to Q, write the question you need to ask to find the object.
- Next to A, write the answer to the question you just asked.
- Circle the type of object it is: direct object (DO), indirect object (IO) or object of a preposition (OP).

1. The children took a shower.

     Q:_____

     A: _____   DO   IO   OP

2. They ate the meal with their friends.

     Q:_____

     A: _____   DO   IO   OP

     Q:_____

     A: _____   DO   IO   OP

3. He sent a present to his brother.

     Q:_____

     A: _____   DO   IO   OP

     Q:_____

     A: _____   DO   IO   OP

WHAT ARE DIRECT AND INDIRECT OBJECT PRONOUNS?

Pronouns used as direct and indirect objects are called **OBJECT PRONOUNS**. 1

> Paul saw *her.*
>> Paul saw whom? ANSWER: Her.
>> *Her* is the object of the verb *saw.*

Pronouns change according to their function in the sentence. Pronouns used as subjects are studied in *What is a Subject Pronoun?*, p. 33. We use subject pronouns when we conjugate verbs (see *What is a Verb Conjugation?*, p. 41). Object pronouns are used when a pronoun is either a direct object, indirect object, or object of a preposition ·(see *What are Objects?*, p. 140; *What are Object of Preposition Pronouns?*, p. 156). 10

IN ENGLISH

Most object pronouns are different from subject pronouns, but the same pronouns are used as direct objects and indirect objects.

	SUBJECT	**OBJECT**
SINGULAR		
1ST PERSON	I	me
2ND PERSON	you	you
3RD PERSON	he	him
	she	her
	it	it
PLURAL		
1ST PERSON	we	us
2ND PERSON	you	you
3RD PERSON	they	them

20

Let us look at a few examples. 30

> She saw *me.*
> direct object → object pronoun

> He lent *me* the car.
> indirect object → object pronoun

As you can see, the object pronoun is always placed after the verb.

IN SPANISH

As in English, the pronouns used as objects are different from the ones used as subjects. Unlike English, however, the form of an object pronoun often changes depending on whether it is a direct or an indirect object.

In Spanish, the direct and indirect object pronouns are usually placed before the verb. Consult your textbook.

SPANISH DIRECT OBJECT PRONOUNS

First, you have to establish that the Spanish verb takes a direct object. Remember that English and Spanish verbs don't always take the same type of objects and that when working in Spanish you have to establish the type of object required by the Spanish verb (see p. 144).

To simplify our examples in this section we have chosen the verb *to see* (**ver**) because both the English and the Spanish verbs take a direct object.

Let us look at the Spanish direct object pronouns to see how they are selected. Since the pattern of the direct object pronouns for *me, you* (**tú** and **vosotros** forms), *him, her* and *us* is different from the pattern for *it, them,* and *you* (**usted** and **ustedes** forms), we have divided the Spanish direct object pronouns into these two categories.

Me, you *(tú* and *vosotros* forms), **him, her, us**

The direct object pronouns equivalent to *me, you, him, her,* and *us* are a question of learning vocabulary. Just select the form you need from the chart below.

DIRECT OBJECTS	
me	me
you [tú form]	te
you [vosotros form]	os
him	lo
her	la
us	nos

Here are some examples.

*John sees **me**.*

1. IDENTIFY THE VERB: *to see* (**ver**)
2. IDENTIFY PRONOUN OBJECT: *me*
3. FUNCTION OF PRONOUN IN SPANISH: direct object
4. SELECTION: **me**

Juan **me** ve.

John sees you.
John **te** ve. [**tú** form]
John **os** ve. [**vosotros** form]

Do you see John? Yes, I see him.
¿Ves a Juan? Sí, **lo** veo.

Do you see Mary? Yes, I see her.
¿Ves a María? Sí, **la** veo.

John sees us.
John **nos** ve.

It, them, you *(usted* and *ustedes* forms)

The direct object pronouns equivalent to *it, them* and *you* change depending on the gender of the ANTECEDENT; that is, the noun which they are replacing.

	DIRECT OBJECTS	
	MASCULINE	FEMININE
it	**lo**	**la**
you [usted form]	**lo**	**la**
them	**los**	**las**
you [ustedes form]	**los**	**las**

Do you see the book? Yes, I see it.
    1. ANTECEDENT: **el libro** *(book)*
    2. GENDER OF ANTECEDENT: masculine
    3. SELECTION: **lo**
¿Ves el libro? Sí, **lo** veo.

Do you see the table? Yes, I see it.
    1. ANTECEDENT: **la mesa** *(table)*
    2. GENDER OF ANTECEDENT: feminine
    3. SELECTION: **la**
¿Ves la mesa? Sí, **la** veo.

Do you see the cars? Yes, I see them.
    1. ANTECEDENT: **los coches** *(cars)*
    2. GENDER OF ANTECEDENT: masculine
    3. SELECTION: **los**
¿Ves los coches? Sí, **los** veo.

Do you see the girls? Yes, I see them.
    1. ANTECEDENT: **las chicas** *(girls)*
    2. GENDER OF ANTECEDENT: feminine
    3. SELECTION: **las**
¿Ves a las chicas? Sí, **las** veo.[1]

---

[1] The "a" before **chicas** is a personal **a**, not a preposition (see p. 141).

The pronoun *you* (formal) changes not only according to the gender of the person or persons you are addressing, but also according to whether you are addressing one or more persons.

> *Whom does John see? He sees **you**.* [when speaking to a male]
>   1. NUMBER & GENDER OF *YOU:* masculine singular
>   2. SELECTION: **lo**
> ¿A quién ve Juan? Juan **lo** ve.

> *Whom does John see? He sees **you**.* [when speaking to a female]
>   1. NUMBER & GENDER OF *YOU:* feminine singular
>   2. SELECTION: **la**
> ¿A quién ve Juan? Juan **la** ve.

> *Whom does John see? He sees **you**.* [when speaking to males or a mixed group]
>   1. NUMBER & GENDER OF *YOU:* masculine plural
>   2. SELECTION: **los**
> ¿A quién ve Juan? Juan **los** ve.

> *Whom does John see? He sees **you**.* [when speaking to females]
>   1. NUMBER & GENDER OF *YOU:* feminine plural
>   3. SELECTION: **las**
> ¿A quién ve Juan? Juan **las** ve.

SPANISH INDIRECT OBJECT PRONOUNS

First, make sure that the Spanish verb takes an indirect object. Remember that English and Spanish verbs don't always take the same type of objects and that when working in Spanish you have to establish the type of object required by the Spanish verb (see p. 144).

To simplify our examples in this section we have chosen the verb *to speak* (**hablar**) because both the English and the Spanish verbs take an indirect object.

Notice that unlike noun indirect objects which are always preceded by "**a**" *(to)* in Spanish (see p. 142), pronoun indirect objects are not.

Let us look at the Spanish indirect object pronouns to see how they are selected. Since the pattern of the indirect object pronouns *me, you* (**tú** and **vosotros** forms), and *us* is different from the pattern of *him, her, you* (**usted** and **ustedes** forms), and *them*, we have divided the Spanish indirect object pronouns into these two categories.

Me, you *(tú* and *vosotros* forms) us

The indirect object pronouns equivalent to *me, you,* and *us* are the same as the direct object pronouns.

INDIRECT OBJECTS	
me	me
you [tú form]	te
us	nos
you [vosotros form]	os

*John speaks **to me**.*
1. IDENTIFY THE VERB: *to speak* (**hablar**)
2. IDENTIFY THE PRONOUN OBJECT: *me*
3. FUNCTION OF THE PRONOUN IN SPANISH: indirect object
4. SELECTION: **me**

Juan **me** habla.

   |

   indirect object pronoun

*John speaks **to you**.*
John **te** habla. [**tú** form]
John **os** habla. [**vosotros** form]

*John speaks **to us**.*
John **nos** habla.

Him, her, you *(usted* and *ustedes* forms), **them**
The indirect object pronouns equivalent to *him, her, you,* and *them* do not distinguish between gender; you can just select the form you need from the chart below.

INDIRECT OBJECTS	
him, her, you [**usted** form]	le
them, you [**ustedes** form]	les

*To whom is John speaking? John is speaking **to him**.*
1. IDENTIFY THE VERB: *to speak* (**hablar**)
2. IDENTIFY THE PRONOUN OBJECT: *him*
3. FUNCTION OF THE PRONOUN IN SPANISH: indirect object
4. SELECTION: **le**

¿A quién **le** habla Juan? Juan **le** habla.[1]

*Are you speaking to Mary? Yes, I am speaking **to her**.*
¿**Le** hablas a María? Sí, **le** hablo.

*To whom is John speaking? He is speaking **to you**.* [one person]
1. IDENTIFY THE VERB: *to speak* (**hablar**)
2. IDENTIFY THE PRONOUN OBJECT: *you*
3. FUNCTION OF PRONOUN IN SPANISH: indirect object
4. SELECTION: **le**

¿A quién **le** habla Juan? **Le** habla.

---

[1]For the inclusion of "**le**" in the question, see p. 142.

*To whom is John speaking? John is speaking **to them**.*
1. IDENTIFY THE VERB: *to speak* (**hablar**)
2. IDENTIFY THE PRONOUN OBJECT: *them*
3. FUNCTION OF PRONOUN IN SPANISH: indirect object
4. SELECTION: **les**

¿A quiénes **les** habla Juan? Juan **les** habla.

*To whom is John speaking? He's speaking **to you**.* [many persons]
1. IDENTIFY THE VERB: *to speak* (**hablar**)
2. IDENTIFY THE PRONOUN OBJECT: *you*
3. FUNCTION OF PRONOUN IN SPANISH: indirect object
4. SELECTION: **les**

¿A quiénes **les** habla Juan? **Les** habla.

In order to distinguish **le** meaning *to him* from **le** meaning *to her* or *to you*, the phrase **a él, a ella**, or **a usted** can be added to the end of the sentence.

> Juan **le** habla **a él**.   *John speaks **to him**.*
> Juan **le** habla **a ella**.   *John speaks **to her**.*
> Juan **le** habla **a usted**. *John speaks **to you**.*

In order to distinguish **les** meaning *to them* (masculine or feminine) and *to you*, the phrase **a ellos, a ellas**, or **a ustedes** can be added to the end of the sentence.

> Juan **les** habla **a ellos**.   *John speaks **to them**.*
>   [group of males or a mixed group]
> Juan **les** habla **a ellas**.   *John speaks **to them**.*
>   [group of females]
> Juan **les** habla **a ustedes**. *John speaks **to you**.*

SUMMARY

As you can see from the various charts in this chapter:

1. The following pronouns have the same form when used as direct and indirect objects.

DIRECT AND INDIRECT OBJECTS	
me	**me**
you [tú form]	**te**
we	**nos**
you [**vosotros** form]	**os**

2. The following pronouns have different forms when used as direct and indirect objects.

	DIRECT OBJECTS	INDIRECT OBJECTS
him	lo	le
her	la	le
it	lo, la	le
you [usted form]	lo, la	le
them	los, las	les
you [ustedes form]	los, las	les

250

3. The following direct object pronouns have a different form depending on the gender of the antecedent.

	DIRECT OBJECTS	
	MASCULINE	FEMININE
it	lo	la
you [usted form]	lo	la
them	los	las
you [ustedes form]	los	las

260

✎ REVIEW

Underline the object pronoun in the sentences below.
- Using the charts on pp. 152-3, circle the correct Spanish equivalent: direct object (DO), or indirect object (IO), singular (S), or plural (P), gender unknown (U) or irrelevant (I).

1. Mary bought the book and then she read it.

FUNCTION OF PRONOUN IN ENGLISH: DO   IO

FUNCTION OF PRONOUN IN SPANISH: DO   IO

ANTECEDENT IN ENGLISH: _____

NUMBER OF ANTECEDENT IN SPANISH: S   P

GENDER OF ANTECEDENT IN SPANISH: masculine

María compró el libro y después _____ leyó.

2. Juan bought some magazines and then he read them.

FUNCTION OF PRONOUN IN ENGLISH: DO   IO

FUNCTION OF PRONOUN IN SPANISH: DO   IO

ANTECEDENT IN ENGLISH: _____

NUMBER OF ANTECEDENT IN SPANISH: S   P

GENDER OF ANTECEDENT IN SPANISH: feminine

Juan compró algunas revistas y después _____ leyó.

3. The teacher spoke to them about the exam yesterday.

FUNCTION OF PRONOUN IN ENGLISH:	DO	IO
FUNCTION OF PRONOUN IN SPANISH:	DO	IO
NUMBER OF ANTECEDENT IN SPANISH:	S	P
GENDER OF ANTECEDENT IN SPANISH:	U	I

La profesora _____ habló del examen ayer.

4. Did you write Paul? No, but I will write him today.

FUNCTION OF PRONOUN IN ENGLISH:	DO	IO
FUNCTION OF PRONOUN IN SPANISH:	DO	IO
NUMBER OF PRONOUN:	S	P
GENDER OF ANTECEDENT IN SPANISH:	masculine	

¿Le escribiste a Pablo? No, pero _____ escribiré hoy.

STUDY TIPS — DIRECT/ INDIRECT OBJECT PRONOUNS

Pattern (see *Tips for Learning Word Forms,* pp. 3-4)

Learn direct object and indirect object pronouns separately.

1. Look for similarities between direct object pronouns and other parts of speech. Refer to the charts on pp. 152-3.

   What similarities can you think of?

   ■ 1st pers. sing. & pl. and 2nd pers. sing. **(me, te, nos)**: initial letters **m-, t-, n-** are the same as possessive adjectives **(mi, tu, nuestro)**

   ■ 3rd pers. fem. sing. & pl. and 3rd pers. masc. pl. **(la, las, los)**: same as definite articles **(la, las, los)**

2. When you learn indirect object pronouns, look for similarities with direct object pronouns as well as other parts of speech.

   What similarities do you notice?

   ■ 1st, 2nd pers. sing. & pl. **(me, te, nos, os)**: same forms for direct and indirect object pronouns

   ■ 3rd pers. sing. & pl. **(le, les)**: same forms for masculine and feminine

   ■ 3rd pers. sing. & pl. **(lo, la, las, los, le, les)**: all begin with letter **l-**

Flashcards

1. On the subject pronoun flashcards, add sentences illustrating the pronoun's form as direct and indirect object.

ella	*she* (subject)
La veo.	*I see **her**.* (direct object)
Le hablo.	*I speak **to her**.* (indirect object)
ellos	*they* (subject, males or mixed group)
Los veo.	*I see **them**.* (direct object)
Les hablo.	*I speak **to them**.* (indirect object)

Practice

1. Since function determines a pronoun's form, it is important to learn direct and indirect object pronouns in a sentence.

2. Write a series of short Spanish sentences with masculine and feminine singular and plural nouns as direct objects. Rewrite the sentences replacing the direct object noun with the appropriate direct object pronoun.

> Juan ve a Susana. *Juan sees Susana.*
> Juan **la** ve. *Juan sees **her**.*

3. Write a series of short Spanish sentences with nouns as indirect objects. Rewrite the sentences replacing the indirect object noun with the appropriate indirect object pronoun.

> Juan le da un regalo a Susana. *Juan gives a gift to Susan.*
> Juan **le** da un regalo. *Juan gives **her** a gift.*

4. In the sentences you've created in No. 3 above replace both the direct object and indirect object nouns with pronouns. (Refer to your textbook for the correct word order.)

> Juan **se lo** da. *Juan gives **it to her**.*

CHAPTER

WHAT ARE OBJECT OF PREPOSITION PRONOUNS?

Object pronouns are also used as
OBJECTS OF A PREPOSITION.

They went out with *me*.
object of preposition *with*

IN ENGLISH

The same forms of object pronouns are used for direct object, indirect object and object of a preposition pronouns (see *What are Direct and Indirect Object Pronouns?*, p. 147).

IN SPANISH

Pronouns that are objects of a preposition other than the preposition *to* (also called **PREPOSITIONAL PRONOUNS**) have forms that are different from the forms used as direct and indirect object pronouns. Object of preposition pronouns are always placed after the preposition.

Let us look at the Spanish object of preposition pronouns to see how they are selected. First, you have to establish that in Spanish there is a preposition, and if so, which one. Remember that English and Spanish verbs do not always use the same preposition, if any, and that when working in Spanish you have to establish the preposition used in Spanish.

To simplify our examples in this section we have chosen English and Spanish verbs that take the same preposition.

Since the pattern of object of preposition pronouns for *me, you* (**tú, usted** and **ustedes** forms), *him*, and *her* is different from the pattern for *us, you* (**vosotros** form), and *them*, we have divided the Spanish object of preposition pronouns into these two categories.

Me, you (tú, usted, ustedes **forms**), **him, her**
The object of preposition pronouns equivalent to *me, you, him, her* are a question of learning vocabulary. Just select the form you need from the following chart.

OBJECTS OF A PREPOSITION	
me	**mí**
you [tú form]	**ti**
him	**él**
her	**ella**
you [usted form]	**usted**
you [ustedes form]	**ustedes**

Here are some examples.

*Is the book for John? No, it's **for me.***
  1. IDENTIFY THE PREPOSITION: *for*
  2. IDENTIFY THE OBJECT OF THE PREPOSITION: *me*
  3. SELECTION: **mí**
¿Es para Juan el libro? No, es **para mí.**

*Is the book for John? Yes, it is **for him.***
  1. IDENTIFY THE PREPOSITION: *for*
  2. IDENTIFY THE OBJECT OF THE PREPOSITION: *him*
  3. SELECTION: **él**
¿Es para Juan el libro? Sí, es **para él.**

*Is the book for Mary? Yes, it is **for her.***
  1. IDENTIFY THE PREPOSITION: *for*
  2. IDENTIFY THE OBJECT OF THE PREPOSITION: *her*
  3. SELECTION: **ella**
¿Es para María el libro? Sí, es **para ella.**

*Is the book for John? No, it's **for you.*** [one person]
  1. IDENTIFY THE PREPOSITION: *for*
  2. IDENTIFY THE OBJECT OF THE PREPOSITION: *you*
  3. DISTINGUISH FORMAL FROM FAMILIAR: familiar
  4. NUMBER OF THE PRONOUN *you*: singular
  5. SELECTION: **ti**
¿Es para Juan el libro? No, es **para ti.**

*Is the book for me? Yes, it is **for you.*** [one person]
  1. IDENTIFY THE PREPOSITION: *for*
  2. IDENTIFY THE OBJECT OF THE PREPOSITION: *you*
  3. DISTINGUISH FORMAL FROM FAMILIAR: formal
  4. NUMBER OF THE PRONOUN *you*: singular
  5. SELECTION: **usted**
¿Es para mí el libro? Sí, es **para usted.**

*Are the books for us? Yes, they're **for you.*** [more than one person]
  1. IDENTIFY THE PREPOSITION: *for*
  2. IDENTIFY THE OBJECT OF THE PREPOSITION: *you*
  3. DISTINGUISH FORMAL FROM FAMILIAR: formal
  4. NUMBER OF THE PRONOUN *you*: plural
  5. SELECTION: **ustedes**
¿Son para nosotros los libros? Sí, son **para ustedes.**

Us, YOU *(vosotros* **form), them**

The object of preposition pronouns equivalent to *us, you,* and *them* change depending on the gender of the persons they refer to.

	OBJECTS OF A PREPOSITION	
	MASCULINE	FEMININE
us	nosotros	nosotras
you	vosotros	vosotras
them	ellos	ellas

*Are the books for John? No, they're **for us.*** [group of males or mixed group]
> 1. IDENTIFY THE PREPOSITION: *for*
> 2. IDENTIFY THE OBJECT OF THE PREPOSITION: *us*
> 3. GENDER OF THE PRONOUN *US*: masculine
> 4. SELECTION: **nosotros**

¿Son para Juan los libros? No, son **para nosotros.**

*Are the books for John? No, they're **for us.*** [group of females]
> 1. - 2. (see above)
> 3. GENDER OF THE PRONOUN *US*: feminine
> 4. SELECTION: **nosotras**

¿Son para Juan los libros? No, son **para nosotras.**

*Are the books for John? No, they're **for you.*** [group of males or mixed group]
> 1. IDENTIFY THE PREPOSITION: *for*
> 2. IDENTIFY THE OBJECT OF THE PREPOSITION: *you*
> 3. DISTINGUISH FORMAL FROM FAMILIAR: familiar
> 4. NUMBER OF THE PRONOUN *YOU*: plural
> 5. GENDER OF THE PRONOUN *YOU*: masculine
> 6. SELECTION: **vosotros**

¿Son para Juan los libros? No, son **para vosotros.**

*Are the books for John? No, they're **for you.*** [group of females]
> 1. - 4. (see above)
> 5. GENDER OF THE PRONOUN *YOU*: feminine
> 6. SELECTION: **vosotras**

¿Son para Juan los libros? No, son **para vosotras.**

*Is the book for the children? Yes, it's **for them.***
> 1. IDENTIFY THE PREPOSITION: *for*
> 2. IDENTIFY THE OBJECT OF THE PREPOSITION: *them*
> 3. GENDER OF THE PRONOUN *THEM*: masculine *(boys)*
> 4. SELECTION: **ellos**

¿Es para los niños el libro? Sí, es **para ellos.**

*Is the book for Mary and Gloria? Yes, it's **for them.***
   1. - 2. (see above)
   3. GENDER OF THE PRONOUN *THEM*: feminine *(Mary and Gloria)*
   4. SELECTION: **ellas**
¿Es para María y Gloria el libro? Sí, es **para ellas.**

CAREFUL — The English object of preposition pronouns for *it* or *them* referring to things has no Spanish equivalent.

✎ REVIEW

Underline the object of preposition pronouns in the sentences below.
- Identify the number of the prepositional pronoun in Spanish: singular (S) or plural (P).
- Identify the gender of the prepositional pronoun in Spanish: masculine (M), feminine (F), gender unknown or doesn't matter (NA).
- Using the charts in this chapter, fill in the blank with the correct form of the prepositional pronoun.

1. Is this gift for Teresa and Ana? Yes, the gift is for them.

   NUMBER OF PREPOSITIONAL PRONOUN IN SPANISH: S   P

   GENDER OF PREPOSITIONAL PRONOUN IN SPANISH: M   F   NA

   ¿Es para Teresa y Ana el regalo? Sí, el regalo es para _____.

2. Is this gift from your mother? Yes, it's from her.

   NUMBER OF PREPOSITIONAL PRONOUN IN SPANISH: S   P

   GENDER OF PREPOSITIONAL PRONOUN IN SPANISH: M   F   NA

   ¿Es este regalo de su madre? Sí, es de _____.

3. Is this letter for John? No, it's for you [tú form].

   NUMBER OF PREPOSITIONAL PRONOUN IN SPANISH: S   P

   GENDER OF PREPOSITIONAL PRONOUN IN SPANISH: M   F   NA

   ¿Es esta carta para Juan? No, es para _____.

4. Is Mary going to the party with John? No, she's going with us.

   NUMBER OF PREPOSITIONAL PRONOUN IN SPANISH: S   P

   GENDER OF PREPOSITIONAL PRONOUN IN SPANISH: M   F   NA

   ¿Va María a la fiesta con Juan? No, va con _____.

Pattern

1. The 1st pers. sing. form has a written accent mark, **mí**.
2. Look for similarities between object of preposition pronouns (charts on pp. 157-8) and other parts of speech with 1st, 2nd and 3rd persons that you've already learned.

	OBJ. OF PREP. PRONOUNS	SUBJECT PRONOUNS	POSSESSIVE ADJECTIVES SING.
SINGULAR			
1st pers.	mí	yo	mi
2nd pers.	ti	tú	tu
3rd pers.	él	él	su
	ella	ella	
	usted	usted	
PLURAL			
1st pers.	nosotros	nosotros	nuestr-
2nd pers.	vosotros	vosotros	vuestr-
3rd pers.	ellos	ellos	su
	ellas	ellas	
	ustedes	ustedes	

What similarities do you notice between object of preposition pronouns and the other parts of speech above?

- all forms except 1st and 2nd pers. sing.: same as subject pronouns
- 1st pers. sing.: only an accent distinguishes the possessive adjective **mi** from the object pronoun **mí**
- 1st pers. pl. and 2nd per. sing. & pl.: initial letter same as initial letter of subject pronoun and possessive adjectives: 1st pers. pl. **n-**, 2nd pers. sing. **t-**, 2nd pers. pl. **v-**

Flashcards

On the subject pronoun flashcards, add sentences illustrating the object of preposition forms.

yo	*I*
Es **para mí**.	*It's **for me**.*
ellas	*them* (group of females)
Es **para ellas**.	*It's **for them**.*

Practice

Create Spanish sentences with a noun object of a preposition. Then, replace the noun with the pronoun.

El regalo es para María.	*The gift is for Mary.*
El regalo es **para ella**.	*The gift is **for her**.*
Carlos vive cerca de Juan.	*Charles lives near John.*
Carlos vive **cerca de él**.	*Charles lives **near him**.*

WHAT ARE REFLEXIVE PRONOUNS AND VERBS?

A **REFLEXIVE VERB** is a verb which is accompanied [1]
by a pronoun, called a **REFLEXIVE PRONOUN**, that serves
"to reflect" the action of the verb back to the subject.

subject = reflexive pronoun → the same person

She *cut herself* with the knife.

reflexive verb

IN ENGLISH

Many regular verbs can take on a reflexive meaning by
adding a reflexive pronoun. [10]

The child *dresses* the doll.

regular verb

The child *dresses herself.*

verb + reflexive pronoun

Reflexive pronouns end with *-self* in the singular and
-selves in the plural.

	SUBJECT PRONOUN	REFLEXIVE PRONOUN
SINGULAR			[20]
1ST PERSON	I	myself
2ND PERSON	you	yourself
3RD PERSON	he	himself
	she	herself
	it	itself
PLURAL		
1ST PERSON	we	ourselves
2ND PERSON	you	yourselves
3RD PERSON	they	themselves

[30]

As the subject changes so does the reflexive pronoun,
because they both refer to the same person or object.

I cut *myself.*
John and Mary blamed *themselves* for the accident.

Although the subject pronoun *you* is the same for the singular and plural, there is a difference in the reflexive pronouns: *yourself* (singular) is used when you are speaking to one person and *yourselves* (plural) is used when you are speaking to more than one.

> *Paul*, did *you* make *yourself* a sandwich?
> *Children*, make sure *you* wash *yourselves* properly.

Reflexive verbs can be in any tense: *I wash myself, I washed myself, I will wash myself*, etc.

IN SPANISH

As in English, Spanish reflexive verbs are formed with a verb and a reflexive pronoun.

Here are the Spanish reflexive pronouns:

SINGULAR		
1ST PERSON	me	*myself*
2ND PERSON	te	*yourself* [**tú** form]
3RD PERSON	se	*himself, herself, yourself* [**usted** form]
PLURAL		
1ST PERSON	nos	*ourselves*
2ND PERSON	os	*yourselves* [**vosotros** form]
3RD PERSON	se	*themselves, yourselves* [**ustedes** form]

In the dictionary, reflexive verbs are listed under the regular verb. For instance, under **lavar** *(to wash)* you will also find **lavarse** *(to wash oneself)*. Notice that the reflexive pronoun **se** is attached to the end of the infinitive to indicate a reflexive verb.

Look at the conjugation of **lavarse**. Notice two things:

1. as in English, the reflexive pronoun changes according to the person of the conjugation
2. unlike English, the reflexive pronoun is placed before the conjugated verb

	SUBJECT PRONOUN +	REFLEXIVE PRONOUN +	VERB
SINGULAR			
1ST PERSON	yo	me	lavo
2ND PERSON	tú	te	lavas
3RD PERSON	él / ella / usted	se	lava

PLURAL

| 1ˢᵀ PERSON | { nosotros / nosotras } | nos lavamos |

2ⁿᵈ PERSON { vosotros / vosotras } os laváis

3ᴿᴰ PERSON { ellos / ellas / ustedes } se lavan

Reflexive verbs can be conjugated in all tenses. The subject pronoun and reflexive pronoun remain the same regardless of the tense of the verb, only the verb form changes: **él se lavará** (future); **él se lavó** (preterite).

Reflexive verbs are common in Spanish. There are many English expressions that are not reflexive in English, but whose Spanish equivalent is a reflexive verb. You will have to memorize such expressions individually.

to wake up	despertarse *(to wake oneself up)*
to get up	levantarse *(to get oneself up)*
to go to bed	acostarse *(to put oneself to bed)*
to go to sleep	dormirse *(to put oneself to sleep)*
to get dressed	vestirse *(to dress oneself)*
to have a good time	divertirse *(to amuse oneself)*
to be worried	preocuparse *(to worry oneself)*

In all the examples above, the Spanish reflexive pronouns have a meaning equivalent to the English reflexive pronouns listed on p. 161 *(myself, yourself, himself,* etc.). This is not always the case. As you will see below, Spanish reflexive pronouns can also indicate reciprocal action.

RECIPROCAL ACTION

IN ENGLISH

To express reciprocal action, that is, an action between two or more persons or things, English uses a regular verb followed by the expression "each other."

The dog and the cat looked at *each other*.
> The expression "each other" tells us that the action of "looking" was reciprocal, i.e. the dog looked at the cat and the cat looked at the dog.

Our children call *each other* every day.
> The expression "each other" tells us that the action of "calling" is reciprocal, i.e. the various children call one another every day.

Reciprocal verbs are always plural since they require that more than one person or thing be involved.

IN SPANISH

Spanish uses reflexive pronouns to express an action that is reciprocal.

> El perro y el gato **se** miraron.
> *The dog and the cat looked at **each other**.*

> Nuestros hijos **se** llaman cada día.
> *Our children call **each other** every day.*

Context will often indicate to you if the meaning of the Spanish pronoun is reflexive *(-self, -selves)* or reciprocal *(each other)*.

> Las chicas **se** miran en el espejo.
>> The information "en el espejo" *(in the mirror)* leads us to believe that the girls are looking at themselves. Therefore, **se** is reflexive.
>
> *The girls look at **themselves** in the mirror.*
> |
>   reflexive

However, when no information is given, the meaning of the Spanish sentence is ambiguous.

> Las chicas **se miran**.
> *The girls **look at themselves**.*   →   REFLEXIVE
> *The girls **look at each other**.*   →   RECIPROCAL

One way to avoid ambiguity, and to indicate that the meaning is reciprocal rather than reflexive, is to add an expression equivalent to "each other," such as "**el uno al otro**" (singular) or "**los unos a los otros**" (plural).

> El perro y el gato **se** miran **el uno al otro**.
> | | |
>   masc. sing. masc. sing.   masc. sing.
> *The dog and the cat look at **each other**.*

> Los niños **se** miran **los unos a los otros**.
> | |
>   masc. pl.   masc. pl.
> *The children look at **each other**.*

Consult your textbook for detailed explanations.

✎ REVIEW

A. Fill in the appropriate English reflexive pronoun in the English sentences.

1. Mary cuts _____ a lot.

   María _____ corta muy a menudo.

2. Mary, you cut _____ a lot.

   María, tú _____ cortas muy a menudo.

3. We dress _____.

   Nosotros _____ vestimos.

4. The children wash_____every evening.

   Los niños _____ lavan todas las noches.

B. Fill in the appropriate English reflexive pronoun or the expression "each other."
   ▪ Circle if the action is reflexive (RX) or if the action is reciprocal (RP).

1. The mother and son kissed _____   RX   RP

2. Ambitious people push _____   RX   RP

   to the limit.

3. To avoid being punished, the boys blamed

   _____ for breaking the glass.   RX   RP

4. When something goes wrong, I always

   blame _____.   RX   RP

5. Do you and your brother write

   _____ on e-mail?   RX   RP

CHAPTER

42

WHAT IS A POSSESSIVE PRONOUN?

A POSSESSIVE PRONOUN is a word that replaces a noun and indicates the possessor of that noun. The word *possessive* comes from *possess,* to own.

Whose house is that? It's *mine.*

replaces the noun *house,* the object possessed, and shows who possesses it, *me*

IN ENGLISH

Here is a list of the possessive pronouns:

SINGULAR POSSESSOR

1ST PERSON		mine
2ND PERSON		yours
3RD PERSON	MASCULINE	his
	FEMININE	hers

PLURAL POSSESSOR

1ST PERSON	ours
2ND PERSON	yours
3RD PERSON	theirs

Possessive pronouns only refer to the possessor, not to the object possessed.

My car is red; what color is John's? *His* is blue.

3rd pers. masc. sing.

John's car is blue. What color is yours? *Mine* is white.

1st pers. sing.

Although the object possessed is the same *(car)*, different possessive pronouns *(his* and *mine)* are used because the possessors are different *(John* and *me).*

Is that John's house? Yes, it is *his.*

Are those John's keys? Yes, they are *his.*

Although the objects possessed are different *(house* and *keys)*, the same possessive pronoun *(his)* is used because the possessor is the same *(John).*

IN SPANISH

Like English, a Spanish possessive pronoun refers to the possessor. Unlike English, and like all Spanish pronouns, it also agrees in gender and number with the ANTECEDENT, that is, with the person or object possessed. In addition, the possessive pronoun is preceded by a definite article that also agrees in gender and number with the antecedent.

Let us look at some English sentences to see how to analyze them in order to find the correct form of the Spanish possessive pronoun.

Where are your books? **Mine** *are in the living room.*

1. Find the possessor (*mine* → 1ˢᵗ person singular).
2. Find the antecedent (*mine* refers to *books*).
3. Establish the gender and number of the Spanish equivalent of the antecedent (*books*).
4. Choose the ending of the possessive pronoun that corresponds in gender and number to step 3 above.
5. Choose the definite article that corresponds in gender and number to step 3 above.

¿Dónde están tus libros? **Los míos** están en la sala.

1. The 1ˢᵗ person singular possessor *(mine)* is indicated by the first two letters of the 1ˢᵗ person singular possessive pronoun → **mí-**.
2. The antecedent is **libros** *(books)*.
3. **Libros** is masculine plural.
4. The masculine plural ending is **-os**.
5. The masculine plural definite article is **los**.

Let us look at the Spanish possessive pronouns to learn how to form them. Each of the possessive pronouns has four forms depending on the gender and number of the antecedent. To choose the proper form follow these steps.

1. Indicate the possessor. This will be shown by the first letters of the possessive pronoun. They are the same initial letters as the stressed possessive adjectives (see *What is a Possessive Adjective?*, p. 118).

SINGULAR POSSESSOR			
1ˢᵀ PERSON		mine	**mí-**
2ᴺᴰ PERSON		yours	**tuy-**
3ᴿᴰ PERSON	MASCULINE	his	
	FEMININE	hers	**suy-**
		yours	

PLURAL POSSESSOR		
1ˢᵀ PERSON	ours	**nuestr-**
2ᴺᴰ PERSON	yours	**vuestr-**
3ᴿᴰ PERSON	theirs	**suy-**
	yours	

2. Establish the gender and number of the antecedent and choose the definite article and the ending that corresponds to its gender and number.

- antecedent is masculine singular → **el** + first letters of the possessor + **-o**

¿Dónde está **el libro?**
       |
  masculine singular

El **mío** está en la mesa.
El **tuyo** está en la mesa.
El **suyo** está en la mesa.
El **nuestro** está en la mesa.
El **vuestro** está en la mesa.
El **suyo** está en la mesa.

*Where is **the book?***

Mine is on the table.
Yours is on the table.
His (hers, yours) is on the table.
Ours is on the table.
Yours is on the table.
Theirs (yours) is on the table.

- antecedent is feminine singular → **la** + first letters of the possessor + **-a**

¿Dónde está **la revista?**
       |
  feminine singular

La **mía** está en la mesa.
La **tuya** está en la mesa.
La **suya** está en la mesa.
La **nuestra** está en la mesa.
La **vuestra** está en la mesa.
La **suya** está en la mesa.

*Where is **the magazine?***

Mine is on the table.
Yours is on the table.
His (hers, yours) is on the table.
Ours is on the table.
Yours is on the table.
Theirs (yours) is on the table.

- antecedent is masculine plural → **los** + first letters of the possessor + **-os**

¿Dónde están **los libros?**
       |
  masculine plural

Los **míos** están en la mesa.
Los **tuyos** están en la mesa.
Los **suyos** están en la mesa.
Los **nuestros** están en la mesa.
Los **vuestros** están en la mesa.
Los **suyos** están en la mesa.

*Where are **the books?***

Mine are on the table.
Yours are on the table.
His (hers, yours) are on the table.
Ours are on the table.
Yours are on the table.
Theirs (yours) are on the table.

- antecedent is feminine plural → **las** + first letters of 120
  the possessor + **-as**

¿Dónde están **las revistas?** **Las mías** están en la mesa.

            |

feminine plural   **Las tuyas** están en la mesa.
                   Las suyas están en la mesa.
                   Las nuestras están en la mesa.
                   Las vuestras están en la mesa.
                   Las suyas están en la mesa.

*Where are **the magazines?*** *Mine are on the table.*
                   Yours are on the table.
                   His (hers, yours) are on the table.
                   Ours are on the table. 130
                   Yours are on the table.
                   Theirs (yours) are on the table.

3. Select the proper form according to the two steps above.

Let us apply these steps to some examples.

*Mary forgot her notebook but we have **ours.***
    1. POSSESSOR: 1ˢᵗ person plural → **nuestr-**
    2. ANTECEDENT: **cuaderno** *(notebook)* → masculine singular
    3. SELECTION: **el** + **nuestr-** + **-o**

María olvidó su cuaderno pero tenemos **el nuestro.**

*I do not have my books, but John and Mary have **theirs.*** 140
    1. POSSESSOR: 3ʳᵈ person plural → **suy-**
    2. ANTECEDENT: **libros** *(books)* → masculine plural
    3. SELECTION: **los** + **suy-** + **-os**

No tengo mis libros pero Juan y María tienen **los suyos.**

*Mary is reading her magazines. John is reading **his.***
    1. POSSESSOR: 3ʳᵈ person singular → **suy-**
    2. ANTECEDENT: **revistas** *(magazines)* → feminine plural
    3. SELECTION: **las** + **suy-** + **-as**

María lee sus revistas. Juan lee **las suyas.**

150

CAREFUL — The definite article is not used when the possessive pronoun follows a form of the verb **ser** *(to be).*

*Is this your coat? No, it's not **mine.** **Mine** is larger.*
¿Es éste tu abrigo? No, no es **mío. El mío** es más grande.
                | └─┬─┘
      possessive pronoun   article + possessive
      without article after **ser**

SUMMARY

Here is a chart you can use as a reference.

160

Singular Possessor		ANTECEDENT	
		Singular	Plural
mine	MASC.	el mío	los míos
	FEM.	la mía	las mías
yours [tú form]	MASC.	el tuyo	los tuyos
	FEM.	la tuya	las tuyas
his, hers, yours [Ud. form]	MASC.	el suyo	los suyos
	FEM.	la suya	las suyas
Plural Possessor		ANTECEDENT	
		Singular	Plural
ours	MASC.	el nuestro	los nuestros
	FEM.	la nuestra	las nuestras
yours [vosotros form]	MASC.	el vuestro	los vuestros
	FEM.	la vuestra	las vuestras
theirs, yours [Uds. form]	MASC.	el suyo	los suyos
	FEM.	la suya	las suyas

170

✎ REVIEW

Underline the possessive pronouns in the sentences below.
- Draw an arrow from the possessive pronoun to its antecedent.
- Circle whether the antecedent is singular (S) or plural (P).
- Using the charts in this section, fill in the Spanish possessive pronoun.

1. I won't take his car. I'll take mine.

ANTECEDENT IN SPANISH: masculine   S   P

No tomaré su coche. Tomaré _____

2. I'm not going with my parents. I'm going with hers.

ANTECEDENT IN SPANISH: masculine   S   P

No voy con mis padres. Voy con _____

3. These aren't your [tú form] boots. Yours are bigger.

ANTECEDENT IN SPANISH: feminine   S   P

No son tus botas. _____ son más grandes.

4. Paul's bicycle is broken. He'll use ours.

ANTECEDENT IN SPANISH: feminine   S   P

La bicicleta de Pablo está rota. Va a usar _____

Pattern

1. It will be easy for you to establish a pattern if you remember that possessive pronouns have the same forms as the stressed possessive adjectives and are used with the corresponding definite article (see *What are Possessive Adjectives*, p. 118).

2. It is the use of the definite article that distinguishes the possessive pronouns from the possessive adjectives.

Flashcards

1. For review, create one card per person (1st, 2nd, 3rd pers. sing. and pl.) with an example of the different forms.

> **el mío,** la mía, los míos, las mías   *mine*

2. On all cards add an example that shows the possessive pronoun without the definite article when it follows the verb **ser** *(to be)*.

> ¿De quíen son estos zapatos?   *Whose shoes are these?*
> No, son **míos. Los míos** son rojos.   *They're not **mine. Mine** are red.*

3. On the cards for the 3rd pers. sing. and pl., to reinforce the fact that **el suyo, la suya, los suyos, las suyas** can mean *his, hers, yours,* and *theirs,* write Spanish questions requiring answers equivalent to *his, hers, yours,* and *theirs.*

> ¿Es el libro de María (Juan)?   *Is it Mary's (John's) book?*
> Sí, es **suyo.**   *Yes, it's **hers (his).***
>
> ¿Son los libros de María (Juan)?   *Are they Mary's (John's) books?*
> Sí, son **suyos.**   *Yes, they're **hers (his).***
>
> ¿Es la casa de Juan y María?   *Is it John's and Mary's house?*
> Sí, es **suya.**   *Yes, it's **theirs.***

Practice

1. Sort out your noun flashcards and select a few masculine and feminine nouns.

2. Look at the Spanish side and go through the cards replacing the nouns with the correct form of the possessive pronoun.

> el coche   *car*
> el mío, el tuyo, el suyo, el nuestro, el vuestro
>
> la casa   *house*
> la mía, la tuya, etc.

3. Write short questions in Spanish requiring an answer with a possessive pronoun.

> ¿Es tu libro?   *Is it your book?*
> Sí, es **mío.**   *Yes, it's **mine.***
>
> ¿Son tus llaves?   *Are they your keys?*
> No, no son **mías.**   *No, they're not **mine.***
>   **Las mías** estan en mi cuarto.   *Mine are in my room.*

4. Give negative answers to the questions you wrote under No. 3 above so that the answer will require a different possessive pronoun from the one given above.

> ¿Es tu libro?   *Is it your book?*
> No, es **suyo.**   *No, it's **his (hers, yours, theirs).***

CHAPTER

WHAT IS AN INTERROGATIVE PRONOUN?

An **INTERROGATIVE PRONOUN** is a word that refers to a noun and introduces a question. The word *interrogative* comes from *interrogate,* to question.

> *Who* is coming for dinner?
> |
> refers to a person

> *What* did you eat for dinner?
> |
> refers to a thing

In both English and Spanish, a different interrogative pronoun is used depending on whether it refers to a "person" (human beings and live animals) or a "thing" (objects and ideas). Also, the form of the interrogative pronoun often changes according to its function in the sentence: subject, direct object, indirect object, and object of a preposition. We shall look at each type separately.

INTERROGATIVE PRONOUNS REFERRING TO A PERSON "WHO, WHOM, WHOSE"
IN ENGLISH

Who is used for the subject of the sentence.

> *Who* lives here?
> |
> subject

> *Who* are they?
> |
> subject

Whom is used for the direct object, indirect object, and object of a preposition.

> *Whom* do you know here?
> |
> direct object

> *To whom* did you speak?
> |
> indirect object

> *From whom* did you get the book?
> |
> object of preposition *from*

Whose is the possessive form and is used to ask about possession or ownership.

There's a pencil on the floor? *Whose* is it?
$$\text{possessive}$$

They are nice cars. *Whose* are they?
$$\text{possessive}$$

IN SPANISH

The interrogative pronoun referring to persons is always **quién** or **quiénes** regardless of its function within the sentence. The use of **quién** or **quiénes** depends on the number of its ANTECEDENT; i.e., the noun the pronoun refers to.

Who or *whom* → **quién** or **quiénes**
Since there is no English equivalent for **quiénes**, both the singular and plural forms translate as *who* or *whom* in English.

- a question with **quién** asks for a singular response
  ¿Quién viene? Juan viene.
  singular subject   singular response
  Who is coming? John is coming.

- a question with **quiénes** asks for a plural response
  ¿Quiénes vienen? Juan, Roberto y Miguel vienen.
  plural subject   plural response
  Who is coming? John, Robert and Michael are coming.

The two examples below require that you restructure the dangling prepositions (see p. 174).

*Who are you leaving **with**? I'm leaving with Robert.* →
***With whom** are you leaving? I'm leaving with Robert.*
  singular   singular response
¿Con quién sales? Salgo con Roberto.

*Who are you leaving **with**? I'm leaving with my friends.* →
***With whom** are you leaving? I'm leaving with my friends.*
  plural   plural response
¿Con quiénes sales? Salgo con mis amigos.

Whose → **de quién** or **de quiénes**
English sentences with *whose* can be re-worded in order to establish the correct word order in Spanish.

1. Replace *whose* with "of whom."

2. Invert the word order of the subject and verb, that is place the verb before the subject.

Whose car is that?
|
(word-for-word: *of whom* is that car)
¿**De quién** es ese coche?

DANGLING PREPOSITIONS
(see *What is a Preposition?*, p. 137)
IN ENGLISH

In English it is difficult to identify the function of pronouns that are objects of a preposition because the pronouns are often separated from the preposition of which they are the object. Consequently, in conversation the interrogative subject pronoun *who* is often used instead of the interrogative object pronoun *whom*.

Who did you give the book *to?*
  | |
interrogative   dangling preposition
pronoun

When a preposition is separated from its object and placed at the end of a sentence or question, it is called a **DANGLING PREPOSITION.**

To enable you to establish the function of an interrogative pronoun, you will have to change the structure of the sentence so that the preposition is placed before the interrogative pronoun. In formal English there is a tendency to avoid dangling prepositions.

SPOKEN ENGLISH	→	FORMAL ENGLISH

Who did you speak *to?*   *To whom* did you speak?
  | |
instead of *whom* preposition

Who did you get the book *from?*   *From whom* did you get the book?
  | |
instead of *whom*   preposition

IN SPANISH

Spanish places prepositions in the same position as formal English; that is, within the sentence or at the beginning of a question. By restructuring English sentences or questions with dangling prepositions you will not only be able to identify the function of interrogative pronouns (and relative pronouns, see p. 183), but also establish the word order for the Spanish sentence.

Here are a few examples of sentences which have been restructured to avoid the dangling preposition.

Who are you writing to? → *To whom are you writing?*
subject form of   preposition   object form of interr. pronoun
interr. pronoun

¿**A quién** le escribes?

Who are you leaving with? → *With whom are you leaving?*
subject form of   preposition   object form of interr. pronoun
interr. pronoun

¿**Con quién** sales?

Who did you buy the gift for? → *For whom did you buy the gift?*
subject form of   preposition   object form of interr. pronoun
interr. pronoun

¿**Para quién** compraste el regalo?

INTERROGATIVE PRONOUN REFERRING TO A THING "WHAT"

IN ENGLISH

What refers only to things or ideas. The same form is used for subject, direct object, indirect object, and the object of a preposition.

What happened?
subject

What do you want?
direct object

What is the movie about?
object of preposition *about*

IN SPANISH

The interrogative pronoun referring to things is always **qué** regardless of its function within the sentence.

What happened?
¿**Qué** pasó?

What do you want?
¿**Qué** quieres?

*What is the movie **about**?* → *About what is the movie?*
¿**De qué** trata la película?

160 **INTERROGATIVE PRONOUNS REQUESTING A SELECTION "WHICH ONE, WHICH ONES"**
IN ENGLISH

Which (one), which (ones) are used in questions that request the selection of one *(which one,* singular) or more than one *(which ones,* plural) from a group that has already been mentioned. The words *one* and *ones* are often omitted from the phrase. These interrogative pronouns can refer to both persons and things and they do not change according to their function.

170 All the teachers are here. *Which one* teaches Spanish?
group   singular subject

I have two cars. *Which one* do you want to take?
group   singular direct object

The library has many books. *Which ones* do you want?
group   plural direct object

He has a group of friends. *Which ones* does he live with?
group   plural object of preposition *with*

180 **IN SPANISH**

As in English these interrogative pronouns do not change according to function. Their form does change, however, according to the number of what you want to say: *which one* (singular) → **cuál** or *which ones* (plural) → **cuáles**.

Which one do you need?
¿**Cuál** necesitas?

Which ones do you need?
¿**Cuáles** necesitas?

190 If the English word *one* or *ones* is not expressed, look at the verb. If the verb is singular, use **cuál**; if the verb is plural, use **cuáles**.

Which of the girls is Spanish?
singular verb
¿**Cuál** de las chicas **es** española?

Which of the girls are Spanish?
plural verb
200 ¿**Cuáles** de las chicas **son** españolas?

CAREFUL — *What is, what are* has two equivalents in Spanish: **qué** + **ser** or **cuál(-es)** + **ser**. To determine which to use you need to decide what the expected answer will be.

- expected answer is a definition → **qué** + **ser**

  > *What is the Nobel Prize?*
  >> The expected answer is a definition of the Nobel Prize.
  >
  > ¿**Qué es** el Premio Nobel?

  > *What are the Panamerican Games?*
  >> The expected answer is a definition of the
  >> Panamerican Games.
  >
  > ¿**Qué son** los Juegos Panamericanos?

- expected answer varies and answers the question *which one(-s)* of many → **cuál(-es)** + **ser**

  > *What is your favorite novel?*
  >> The expected answer will explain which novel
  >> of the many that exist is the favorite.
  >
  > ¿**Cuál es** su novela favorita?

  > *What are the countries of Europe?*
  >> The expected answer will explain which countries
  >> of the many in the world are European.
  >
  > ¿**Cuáles son** los países de Europa?

There is another interrogative pronoun that we will now examine separately since it does not follow the same pattern as above.

"HOW MUCH, HOW MANY"
IN ENGLISH

The English interrogative pronouns *how much, how many* are a rare example of English pronouns that change to agree in number with the noun they replace.

> I have money. *How much* do you need?
> singular   singular
> noun   pronoun

> I have some stamps. *How many* do you need?
> plural   plural
> noun   pronoun

IN SPANISH

This interrogative pronoun has four forms that change according to the gender and number of the ANTECEDENT, that is, the noun replaced by the pronoun.

	SINGULAR *how much*	PLURAL *how many*
MASCULINE	cuánto	cuántos
FEMININE	cuánta	cuántas

To choose the proper form, follow these steps:

1. Determine the antecedent.
2. Determine the gender of the antecedent.
3. Determine the number of the antecedent.

Let us apply these steps to some examples.

I have a lot of paper. **How much** *do you want?*
  1. ANTECEDENT: **el papel** *(paper)*
  2. GENDER OF ANTECEDENT: masculine
  3. NUMBER OF ANTECEDENT: singular
  4. SELECTION: **cuánto**

Tengo mucho papel. ¿**Cuánto** quieres?

I have a lot of meat. **How much** *do you want?*
  1. ANTECEDENT: **la carne** *(meat)*
  2. GENDER OF ANTECEDENT: feminine
  3. NUMBER OF ANTECEDENT: singular
  4. SELECTION: **cuánta**

Tengo mucha carne. ¿**Cuánta** quieres?

I have a lot of books. **How many** *do you want?*
  1. ANTECEDENT: **los libros** *(books)*
  2. GENDER OF ANTECEDENT: masculine
  3. NUMBER OF ANTECEDENT: plural
  4. SELECTION: **cuántos**

Tengo muchos libros. ¿**Cuántos** quieres?

I have a lot of magazines. **How many** *do you want?*
  1. ANTECEDENT: **las revistas** *(magazines)*
  2. GENDER OF ANTECEDENT: feminine
  3. NUMBER OF ANTECEDENT: plural
  4. SELECTION: **cuántas**

Tengo muchas revistas. ¿**Cuántas** quieres?

✎ REVIEW

A. Underline the interrogative pronouns in the questions below.

- Circle the function of the interrogative pronoun in the Spanish sentence: subject (S), object (O), or possessive (P).
- Fill in the Spanish equivalent of the interrogative.

1. *Whose* sweater is this?

   FUNCTION: S   O   P

   RESTRUCTURE THE SENTENCE: _____

   ¿ _____ es este suéter?

2. *Who* are you talking to?

   FUNCTION: S   O   P

   RESTRUCTURE THE SENTENCE: _____

   ¿A _____ le hablas?

3. *Who* is coming to see you? My friends.

   FUNCTION: S   O   P

   ¿ _____ vienen a verte? Mis amigos.

STUDY TIPS — INTERROGATIVE PRONOUNS

Pattern (see *Tips for Learning Word Forms,* pp. 3-4)
Flashcards
For review, create a card with a short question illustrating each form.

         quién, quiénes   *who, whom*

Practice
1. On a blank piece of paper write questions using the various Spanish forms.
2. Write Spanish sentences answering questions with "who," "what," "how much" and "how many." Then write the questions for your answers.

   ANSWER: **Los estudiantes** estudian en la biblioteca.
   The students study in the library.

   QUESTION: ¿**Quiénes** estudian en la biblioteca?
   Who studies in the library?

   ANSWER: Escriben **una carta.**
   They are writing a letter.

   QUESTION: ¿**Qué** escriben?
   What are they writing?

   ANSWER: Compraron **ocho** discos nuevos.
   They bought eight new CDs.

   QUESTION: ¿**Cuántos** discos nuevos compraron?
   How many CDs did they buy?

CHAPTER

WHAT IS A DEMONSTRATIVE PRONOUN?

A **DEMONSTRATIVE PRONOUN** is a word that replaces a noun as if pointing to it. The word *demonstrative* comes from *demonstrate*, to show.

Choose a suit. *This one* is expensive. *That one* is not.
antecedent   points to one suit   points to another suit

In English and Spanish, demonstrative pronouns can be used in a variety of ways.

"THIS ONE, THAT ONE" AND "THESE, THOSE"
IN ENGLISH

The singular demonstrative pronouns are **this (one)** and **that (one)**; the plural forms are **these** and **those**.

Here are my suitcases. *This one* is big; *those* are small.
antecedent   singular   plural

Choose a book. *Those* are in Spanish; *that one* is in English.
antecedent plural   singular

This (one), *these* refer to persons or objects near the speaker, and *that (one)*, *those* refer to persons or objects further away from the speaker.

This and *that* are also used to refer to an unspecified object, idea, or previous statement.

What is *that?*
the object pointed to is unspecified

That is true.
refers to an idea previously expressed

IN SPANISH

Demonstrative pronouns agree in gender with their **ANTECEDENT**; that is, the noun to which they refer. Their number depends on whether they refer to one person or object *(this one, that one)* or to more than one person or object *(these, those)*. Demonstrative pronouns are the same words as demonstrative adjectives, except that all pronoun forms carry a written accent mark in order to distinguish the pronouns from the adjectives (see pp. 129-31).

As pronouns, these words replace the demonstrative adjective + noun; they agree in number and gender with the noun replaced.

Here is a chart you can use as reference.

TO POINT OUT:	SINGULAR		PLURAL	
	MASCULINE	FEMININE	MASCULINE	FEMININE
ITEMS NEAR THE SPEAKER	éste	ésta	éstos	éstas
	this (one)		*these*	
ITEMS NEAR THE THE PERSON SPOKEN TO	ése	ésa	ésos	ésas
	that (one)		*those*	
ITEMS AWAY FROM THE SPEAKER AND PERSON SPOKEN TO	aquél	aquélla	aquéllos	aquéllas
	that one (over there)		*those (over there)*	

To choose the correct form, follow these steps.

1. Determine the location of the item pointed out in relation to the speaker or person spoken to.
2. Find the antecedent.
3. Determine the gender of the antecedent.
4. Determine the number of the antecedent: *this one, that one* → singular; *these, those* → plural.
5. Based on Steps 2, 3 and 4, choose the correct word from the chart above.

Let us apply these steps to some examples.

> *Which book do you want?* ***This one.***
> 1. RELATIONSHIP: near the speaker
> 2. ANTECEDENT: *book* (**libro**)
> 3. GENDER OF THE ANTECEDENT: **libro** → masculine
> 4. NUMBER OF THE ANTECEDENT: *this one* → singular
> 5. SELECTION: **éste**

¿Qué libro quieres? **Éste.**

> *Which magazine do you want?* ***That one.***
> 1. RELATIONSHIP: near the person spoken to
> 2. ANTECEDENT: *magazine* (**revista**)
> 3. GENDER OF THE ANTECEDENT: **revista** → feminine
> 4. NUMBER OF THE ANTECEDENT: *that one* → singular
> 5. SELECTION: **ésa**

¿Qué revista quieres? **Ésa.**

Which notebooks do you want? Those (over there).
    1. RELATIONSHIP: away from the speaker and the person spoken to
    2. ANTECEDENT: *notebooks* (**cuadernos**)
    3. GENDER OF THE ANTECEDENT: **cuadernos** → masculine
    4. NUMBER OF THE ANTECEDENT: *those* → plural
    5. SELECTION: **aquéllos**
¿Qué cuadernos quieres? **Aquéllos.**

Which suitcases do you want? These.
    1. RELATIONSHIP: near the speaker
    2. ANTECEDENT: *suitcases* (**maletas**)
    3. GENDER OF THE ANTECEDENT: **maletas** → feminine

    4. NUMBER OF THE ANTECEDENT: *these* → plural
    5. SELECTION: **éstas**
¿Qué maletas quieres? **Éstas.**

SPANISH NEUTER DEMONSTRATIVE PRONOUNS

Spanish also has three demonstrative pronouns that are used to refer to an unspecified object, idea, or previous statement. These pronouns are said to be NEUTER; that is, they have no gender or their gender is not known. These pronouns are INVARIABLE; that is, they do not change form.

esto	*this (one)*
eso	*that (one)*
aquello	*that (one over there)*

Let us look at some examples of these neuter demonstrative pronouns.

*What is **this**?*
    Since the antecedent of "this" is unknown, the gender and number of the antecedent is also unknown. The neuter form must be used.
¿Qué es **esto**?

***That's** not true.*
    The antecedent of "that" is a previous statement which has no gender. The neuter form must be used.
Eso no es verdad.

*What is **that over there**?*
    Since the antecedent of "that over there" is unknown, the gender and number of the antecedent is also unknown. The neuter form must be used.
¿Qué es **aquello**?

✎ **REVIEW**

Circle the demonstrative pronouns in the following sentences.
- Circle if the item pointed to is near the speaker (NS), near the person spoken to (NPS), or away from both (A).
- Draw an arrow from the demonstrative pronoun to its antecedent.
- Circle if the antecedent is singular (S) or plural (P).
- Fill in the Spanish demonstrative pronoun in the Spanish sentences (see chart p. 181).

1. She did not buy that dress because she wants this one.

      RELATIONSHIP TO SPEAKER: NS   NPS   A

      ANTECEDENT IN SPANISH: masculine   S   P

    Ella no compró ese vestido porque quiere _____.

2. Which notebook is yours? That one.

      RELATIONSHIP TO SPEAKER: NS   NPS   A

      ANTECEDENT IN SPANISH: masculine   S   P

    ¿Qué cuaderno es tuyo? _____.

3. These new houses are more expensive than those over there.

      RELATIONSHIP TO SPEAKER: NS   NPS   A

      ANTECEDENT IN SPANISH: feminine   S   P

    Estas casas nuevas son más caras que _____.

CHAPTER

WHAT IS A RELATIVE PRONOUN?

A **RELATIVE PRONOUN** is a word used at the beginning of a clause giving additional information about someone or something previously mentioned.

clause
additional information about *the book*
I'm reading the book *that* the teacher recommended.

A relative pronoun serves two purposes:

1. As a pronoun it stands for a noun previously mentioned. The noun to which it refers is called the **ANTECEDENT**.

This is the boy *who* broke the window.
antecedent of the relative pronoun *who*

2. It introduces a **SUBORDINATE CLAUSE**; that is, a group of words having a subject and a verb which cannot stand alone because it does not express a complete thought. A subordinate clause is dependent on a **MAIN CLAUSE**; that is, another group of words having a subject and a verb which can stand alone as a complete sentence.

main clause   subordinate clause
Here comes the boy *who broke the window.*
verb   subject   subject   verb

A subordinate clause that starts with a relative pronoun is also called a **RELATIVE CLAUSE**. In the example above, the relative clause starts with the relative pronoun *who* and gives us additional information about the antecedent *boy.*

Relative clauses are very common. We use them in everyday speech without giving much thought as to why and how we construct them. The relative pronoun allows us to combine two thoughts which have a common element into a single sentence.

SENTENCE A   I met the teacher.
SENTENCE B   He teaches Spanish.
COMBINED   I met the teacher *who* teaches Spanish.

When sentences are combined with a relative pronoun, the relative pronoun can have different functions in the relative clause. It can be the subject, the direct object, the indirect object or the object of a preposition.

The selection of a relative pronoun often depends not only on its function in the relative clause, but also on whether its antecedent is a "person" (human beings and animals) or a "thing" (objects and ideas).

IN ENGLISH

In an English sentence, relative pronouns can sometimes be omitted.

> The book *that* I'm reading is interesting.
> |
>   relative pronoun

> The book I'm reading is interesting.
> |
> relative pronoun omitted

IN SPANISH

The main difference between Spanish and English relative pronouns is that relative pronouns must always be expressed in Spanish sentences.[1]

Since the selection of a relative pronoun depends on its function in the relative clause, we shall look at each function separately.

SUBJECT OF THE RELATIVE CLAUSE

(see *What is a Subject?*, p. 29)

IN ENGLISH

There are three relative pronouns that can be used as subjects of a relative clause, depending on whether the relative pronoun refers to a person or a thing. When it is the subject of a relative clause, a relative pronoun is never omitted.

1. PERSON — *Who* or *that* is used as subject of the relative clause.

> She is the only student *who* answered all the time.
> She is the only student *that* answered all the time.
> | |
>   antecedent   relative pronoun
>   subject of *answered*

---

[1]This handbook will not deal with the forms of **el que, el cual,** or **cuyo** since they are not included in most beginning textbooks.

80   2. THING — *Which* or *that* is used as subject of the relative clause.

> The movie *which* is so popular was filmed in Spain.
> The movie *that* is so popular was filmed in Spain.
>
> antecedent   relative pronoun
>   subject of *is*

Notice that the relative pronoun subject is always followed by a verb.

IN SPANISH

90   There is only one relative pronoun that can be used as subject of a relative clause: **que**.

1. & 2. PERSON OR THING — **Que** is used as the subject of a relative clause.

> *John is the student **who (that)** answered.*
> Juan es el estudiante **que** respondió.
>
> *Here is the phone **which (that)** isn't working.*
> Aquí está el teléfono **que** no funciona.

COMBINING SENTENCES: RELATIVE PRONOUN SUBJECT

100   **IN ENGLISH**

> SENTENCE A   The students received good grades.
> SENTENCE B   They studied.

1. Identify the element the two sentences have in common.

> Both *the students* and *they* refer to the same persons.

2. The common element in the first sentence is called the **ANTECEDENT** of the relative pronoun; that is, the person or thing to which the relative pronoun refers. The relative pronoun always replaces the common element in
110   the second sentence.

> *The students* is the antecedent.
> *They* will be replaced by a relative pronoun.

3. The relative pronoun in the relative clause has the same function as the word it replaces.

> *They* is the subject of *studied.* Therefore,
> the relative pronoun will be the subject of *studied.*

4. Choose the relative pronoun according to whether its antecedent is a person or a thing.

120
> *They* refers to *students.* Therefore, its antecedent
> is a person.

5. Select the relative pronoun.

> *Who* or *that* is the subject relative pronoun
> referring to a person.

6. Place the relative pronoun at the beginning of the second sentence, thus forming a relative clause.

> *who* studied
> *that* studied

7. Place the relative clause right after its antecedent.

> The students **who** *studied received good grades.*
> The students **that** *studied received good grades.*
> | |
> antecedent relative clause

130

IN SPANISH

> SENTENCE A   Los estudiantes recibieron buenas notas.
> SENTENCE B   Estudiaron.

Follow the same steps as under In English above, skipping step 4.

> Los estudiantes **que** estudiaron recibieron buenas notas.
> | |
> antecedent   relative clause

140

DIRECT OBJECT OF THE RELATIVE CLAUSE

(see pp. 140-1 in *What are Direct and Indirect Objects?*)

IN ENGLISH

There are three relative pronouns that can be used as direct objects of a relative clause, depending on whether the relative pronoun refers to a person or a thing. When it is the direct object of a relative clause, a relative pronoun is often omitted.

150

1. PERSON — **Whom** or **that** is used as direct object of a relative clause.

> This is the student *(whom)* I saw yesterday.
> This is the student *(that)* I saw yesterday.
> | |
> antecedent   direct object of *saw*

2. THING — **Which** or **that** is used as direct object of a relative clause.

> This is the book *(which)* Paul bought.
> This is the book *(that)* Paul bought.
> | |
> antecedent direct object of *bought*

160

Notice that when expressed the relative pronoun direct object is always followed by a noun or pronoun.

IN SPANISH

There is only one relative pronoun that can be used as direct object of a relative clause: **que.** Unlike English the relative pronoun is never omitted.

1. & 2. PERSON OR THING — **Que** is used as direct object of a relative clause.

We have included the relative pronouns in the English sentences below to show you what the Spanish relative pronoun relates to; however, since relative pronouns are often omitted in English, we have put them between parentheses.

> *This is the student (**whom**) John saw last night.*
> Este es el estudiante **que** Juan vio anoche.

> *This is the book (**that**) John bought.*
> Este es el libro **que** Juan compró.

COMBINING SENTENCES: RELATIVE PRONOUN DIRECT OBJECT
IN ENGLISH

> SENTENCE A　The Spanish teacher is nice.
> SENTENCE B　I met her today.

> 1. COMMON ELEMENT: *Spanish teacher* and *her*
> 2. ELEMENT TO BE REPLACED: *her*
> 3. FUNCTION OF *HER*: direct object
> 4. ANTECEDENT: *the Spanish teacher* is a person.
> 5. SELECTION: *whom* or *that*
> 6. RELATIVE CLAUSE: *whom (that) I met today*
> 7. PLACEMENT: antecedent (*the Spanish teacher*) + relative clause

*The Spanish teacher (**whom**) I met today is nice.*
*The Spanish teacher (**that**) I met today is nice.*
　　　　　　　　|　　　　　　　|
　　　antecedent　　　relative clause

When the relative pronoun *whom* or *that* is left out ("The Spanish teacher I met today is nice"), it is difficult to identify the two clauses.

IN SPANISH

> SENTENCE A　La profesora de español es simpática.
> SENTENCE B　La conocí hoy.

Follow the same steps as under In English above, skipping step 4.

La profesora de español **que** conocí hoy es simpática.
　　　|　　　　　　　　　　　|
　antecedent　　　　　　relative clause

INDIRECT OBJECT AND OBJECT OF A PREPOSITION
IN A RELATIVE CLAUSE

(see pp. 141-4 in *What are Direct and Indirect Objects?*)

Both the relative pronoun as an indirect object and the relative pronoun as an object of a preposition involve prepositions. 210

> Mary is the person to *whom* he gave the present.
> |
> relative pronoun indirect object (object of preposition *to*)

> Mary is the person with *whom* he went out.
> |
> relative pronoun object of the preposition *with*

IN ENGLISH

It is difficult to identify the function of these relative pronouns because they are often separated from the preposition of which they are the object. When a preposition is separated from its object and placed at the end of a sentence it is called a **DANGLING PREPOSITION** (see p. 174). 220

> Mary is the person *that* he went out *with*.
> | |
> relative pronoun   dangling preposition

There are two relative pronouns used as indirect objects or as objects of a preposition in a relative clause, depending on whether the relative pronoun refers to a person or a thing. When it is the indirect object or the object of a preposition in a relative clause, a relative pronoun is often omitted. 230

1. PERSON — ***Whom*** is used as indirect object and as object of a preposition.

> Here is the student to *whom* I was speaking.
> | |
> antecedent   indirect object (object of preposition *to*)

> Here is the student about *whom* I was speaking.
> | |
> antecedent   object of preposition *about*

The above sentences are usually expressed as follows: 240

> Here is the student I was speaking *to*.
> Here is the student I was speaking *about*.

These sentences without a relative pronoun and with a dangling preposition have to be restructured in order to establish the function of the relative pronoun in the Spanish sentences. To restructure the English sentences, follow these steps.

1. Identify the antecedent.
2. Place the preposition after the antecedent.
3. Add the relative pronoun *whom* after the preposition.

SPOKEN ENGLISH →	RESTRUCTURED
Here is the student	Here is the student
I was speaking *to*.	*to whom* I was speaking.

indirect object (object of preposition *to*)

Here is the student	Here is the student
I was speaking *about*.	*about whom* I was speaking.

object of preposition *about*

2. THING — **Which** is used as indirect object and as object of a preposition.

Here is the museum he gave the painting *to*.

antecedent   dangling preposition

SPOKEN ENGLISH →	RESTRUCTURED
Here is the museum	Here is the museum
he gave the painting *to*.	*to which* he gave the painting.

indirect object (object of preposition *to*)

IN SPANISH

The choice of the relative pronoun used as an indirect object or as an object of a preposition depends on whether the relative pronoun refers to a person or a thing. Unlike English, the relative pronoun is never omitted.

1. PERSON — **Quien** or **quienes** is used as the indirect object and as object of a preposition of a relative clause. You will often need to restructure the English sentence before attempting to put it into Spanish.

SPOKEN ENGLISH →	RESTRUCTURED
John is the boy	*John is the boy*
*I'm going **with**.*	*__with whom__ I'm going.*

preposition   object of preposition *with*

Juan es el chico **con quien** salgo.

SPOKEN ENGLISH →	RESTRUCTURED
The girls I'm writing	*The girls*
to live in Madrid.	*__to whom__ I'm writing live in Madrid.*

preposition   object of preposition *to*

Las chicas **a quienes** les escribo viven en Madrid.

2. THING — In conversational Spanish a preposition + **que** is generally used.

SPOKEN ENGLISH	→	RESTRUCTURED
This is the book		*This is the book*
*I was talking **about**.*		***about which** I was talking.*

preposition   object of preposition *about*

Este es el libro **de que** hablaba.

300

SUMMARY

Here is a chart you can use as reference:

FUNCTION IN RELATIVE CLAUSE:	ANTECEDENT	
	PERSON	THING
SUBJECT	*who, that* que	*that, which* que
DIRECT OBJECT	*whom, that* que	*that, which* que
INDIRECT OBJECT OBJECT OF PREPOSITION	*whom, that* quien(-es)	*that, which* que

310

As you can see, Spanish relative pronouns are relatively easy: basically **que** is used in all cases and for all functions, except indirect objects and objects of a preposition referring to persons when Spanish uses **quien** or **quienes**. The difficulty arises from the English usage of relative pronouns. Your ability to handle Spanish relative pronouns correctly will depend on two factors: 1. reinstating relative pronouns which are often omitted in English and 2. restructuring English dangling prepositions.

320

To find the appropriate Spanish relative pronoun you must go through the following steps.

1. Find the relative clause.
   - Restructure the English clause if there is a dangling preposition.
   - Add the relative pronoun if it has been omitted.

2. Establish the function of the relative pronoun in the Spanish sentence:

330

SUBJECT — If the relative pronoun is the subject of the English sentence, it will be the subject of the Spanish sentence → **que**.

DIRECT OBJECT — If the Spanish verb takes a direct object → **que**.

INDIRECT OBJECT OR OBJECT OF A PREPOSITION — Establish whether the relative pronoun refers to a person or a thing.

- a person → preposition + **quien** (sing.) or preposition + **quienes** (pl.)
- a thing → preposition + **que**

3. Based on step 2 select the Spanish form (see p. 191).
4. Place the relative pronoun and its clause right after the antecedent.

Let's apply the steps outlined above to the following sentences:

*The lady **who** is my neighbor is from Colombia.*
　1. RELATIVE CLAUSE: who is my neighbor
　2. ANTECEDENT: *lady* (**señora**)
　3. FUNCTION OF RELATIVE PRONOUN IN SPANISH: subject of relative clause
　4. SELECTION: **que**
　5. PLACEMENT: antecedent *(señora)* + **que** + clause
La señora **que** es mi vecina es de Colombia.

*Here are the books **(that)** I bought yesterday.*
　1. RELATIVE CLAUSE: that I bought yesterday
　2. ANTECEDENT: *books* (**libros**)
　3. FUNCTION OF RELATIVE PRONOUN IN SPANISH: direct object of **comprar** *(to buy)*
　4. SELECTION: **que**
　5. PLACEMENT: antecedent *(libros)* + **que** + clause
Aquí están los libros **que** compré ayer.

*Peter and Joe are the boys I was talking **to**.* →
RESTRUCTURE: *Peter and Joe are the boys **to whom** I was talking.*
　1. RELATIVE CLAUSE: to whom I was talking
　2. ANTECEDENT: *boys* (**chicos**)
　3. FUNCTION OF RELATIVE PRONOUN IN SPANISH: object of preposition *to*
　4. SELECTION: **quienes**
　5. PLACEMENT: antecedent *(chicos)* + **a quienes** + clause
Pedro y José son los chicos **a quienes** hablaba.

Relative pronouns can be tricky to handle and this handbook provides only a simple outline. Refer to your Spanish textbook for additional rules.

RELATIVE PRONOUNS WITHOUT ANTECEDENTS

There are relative pronouns that do not refer to a specific noun or pronoun. Instead, they refer to an antecedent which has not been expressed or to an entire idea.

IN ENGLISH

There are two relative pronouns that can be used without an antecedent: *what* and *which.*

What — does not refer to a specific noun or pronoun.   380

> I don't know *what* happened.
> |
> no antecedent
> subject

> Here is *what* I read.
> |
> no antecedent
> direct object

Which — refers to an entire idea, not to a specific noun or pronoun.   390

> She didn't do well, *which* is too bad.
> |
> antecedent: the fact that she didn't do well
> subject of *is*

> You speak many languages, *which* I envy.
> |
> antecedent: the fact that you speak many languages
> direct object of *envy (I* is the subject)

IN SPANISH

When a relative pronoun does not have a specific antecedent, the pronoun **lo que** is used. It is used in con-   400
versational Spanish and refers to an idea or previously mentioned statement or concept that has no gender. It can function as a subject or object.

Here are a few examples.

What bothers me most is the heat.
1. RELATIVE CLAUSE: what bothers me most
2. ANTECEDENT: none expressed in the sentence
3. FUNCTION OF RELATIVE PRONOUN IN SPANISH: subject of relative clause
4. SELECTION: **lo que**   410

Lo que me molesta más es el calor.

What you are saying isn't true.
1. RELATIVE CLAUSE: what you are saying
2. ANTECEDENT: none expressed in the sentence
3. FUNCTION OF RELATIVE PRONOUN IN SPANISH: direct object of **decir** *(to say)*
4. SELECTION: **lo que**

Lo que dices no es verdad.

*He doesn't speak Spanish, **which** will be a problem.*

420

   1. RELATIVE CLAUSE: which will be a problem

   2. ANTECEDENT: entire previous clause, *he doesn't speak Spanish*

   3. FUNCTION OF RELATIVE PRONOUN IN SPANISH: subject of relative clause

   4. SELECTION: **lo que**

No habla español **lo que** será un problema.

✎ REVIEW

Underline the relative pronoun in the sentences below.

- Circle the antecedent or (NA) if there is no antecedent.
- Circle the function of the relative pronoun: subject (S), direct object (DO), indirect object (IO), object of a preposition (OP), or possessive (P).
- Using the chart on p. 191, fill in the Spanish relative pronoun in the Spanish sentences below.

1. I received the letter that you sent me.   NA

   *(to send → **enviar**)*

      FUNCTION IN SPANISH: S   DO   IO   OP   P

   Recibí la carta _____ me enviaste.

2. That is the woman who speaks Spanish.   NA

      FUNCTION IN SPANISH: S   DO   IO   OP   P

   Esa es la mujer _____ habla español.

3. Paul is the student I traveled with.   NA

      RESTRUCTURE:

   _____

      FUNCTION IN SPANISH: S   DO   IO   OP   P

   Pablo es el estudiante con _____ viajé.

4. What he said was a lie.   NA

      FUNCTION IN SPANISH: S   DO   IO   OP   P

   _____ dijo fue una mentira.

CHAPTER

WHAT ARE INDEFINITES AND NEGATIVES?

Words that refer to persons, things, or periods of time that
are not specific or that are not clearly
defined are called **INDEFINITES**.

There was *someone* in the kitchen.
|
refers to a person that is not specified → indefinite word

Words that deny the existence of persons, things, or
periods of time or that contradict ideas or
previous statements are called **NEGATIVES**.

There was *no one* in the kitchen.
|
denies the existence of a person → negative word

IN ENGLISH

Some common indefinites are *someone, anybody, something, someday.* These indefinite words are often paired
with negative words which are opposite in meaning: *no
one, nobody, nothing,* and *never.*

INDEFINITES	NEGATIVES
someone anyone	*no one*
somebody anybody	*nobody*
something anything	*nothing*
someday any day	*never*

In conversation indefinites frequently appear in questions
while negatives appear in answers.

QUESTION: Is *anyone* coming tonight?
ANSWER: *No one.*

QUESTION: Do you have *anything* for me?
ANSWER: *Nothing.*

QUESTION: Are you going to Europe *someday*?
ANSWER: *Never.*

English sentences can be made negative in one of two ways.

- the word ***not*** appears before the main verb (see *What are Affirmative and Negative Sentences?*, p. 53)

> He is *not* working today.
> I am *not* studying.

- a negative word can be used in any part of the sentence

> *No one* is coming.
> He has *never* seen a movie.

English allows only one negative word (either *not* or any of the other negative words) in a sentence. When a sentence contains the word *not*, another negative word cannot be used in that sentence.

> "I am *not* studying *nothing*" [incorrect English]
> | |
>   *not*   negative word
> This sentence contains a double negative: *not* and *nothing*.

When a sentence contains the word *not*, the indefinite word that is the opposite of the negative word must be used (see chart p. 195).

> I am *not* studying *anything*.
> |
> indefinite word opposite of negative word *nothing*

Let us look at another example.

> I have said *nothing* to them.
> |
>   negative word
> *Nothing* is the one negative word.

> I have *not* said *anything* to them.
> |
>   indefinite word
> This sentence contains *not*; therefore, the word *anything* is substituted for *nothing*.

> "I have *not* said *nothing*" [incorrect English]
> This sentence contains a double negative: *not* and *nothing*.

IN SPANISH

As in English, the indefinite and negative words exist as pairs of opposites. Here is a chart of the most common indefinites and negatives.

INDEFINITES		NEGATIVES	
something	**algo**	**nada**	*nothing*
some, any	**algún** **alguno**	**ningún** **ninguno**	*none*
someone *somebody*	**alguien**	**nadie**	*no one* *nobody*
someday *always* *sometimes*	**algún día** **siempre** **a veces**	**nunca**	*never*
also, too	**también**	**tampoco**	*not...either*
either, or	**o**	**ni**	*neither...nor*

Contrary to English, an indefinite word cannot appear in a negative Spanish sentence. A negative word, not an indefinite, is used in a Spanish sentence that contains **no** meaning *not*.

No tengo **nada**.
  | |
not + negative word *(nothing)*

*I do **not** have **anything**.*
      | |
not + indefinite word *(anything)*

The following formula for indefinites and negatives in English and Spanish will help you use them correctly.

ENGLISH →   *not* + main verb + indefinite word(s)
SPANISH →   no + verb + negative word(s)

As you can see from the formula above, Spanish requires two negatives in the same sentence. A construction that would be incorrect in English.

No veo a **nadie**.
 | |
no + negative word
[word-for-word: *I do **not** see **nobody**]*

*I do **not** see **anybody**.*
   | |
not + indefinite word

120 Follow these steps to find the Spanish equivalent of an English sentence with *not* + an indefinite word:

1. Locate the indefinite word in the English sentence.
2. From the chart on p. 195 choose the negative word that is the opposite of the English indefinite word.
3. Restructure the English sentence using *not* + the negative word chosen under 2 above.
4. Put the sentence into Spanish.

Let us apply the steps above to the following sentences.

130
> *I do **not** want to eat **anything**.*
> > 1. IDENTIFY THE INDEFINITE: anything
> > 2. SELECT THE NEGATIVE: nothing
> > 3. RESTRUCTURE: "I do *not* want to eat *nothing*"
>
> **No** quiero comer **nada**.

> *I don't (not) know **anyone** here.*
> > 1. IDENTIFY THE INDEFINITE: anyone
> > 2. SELECT THE NEGATIVE: no one
> > 3. RESTRUCTURE: "I don't know *no one* here"
>
> **No** conozco a **nadie** aquí.

 REVIEW

Underline the indefinite word or phrase in the following sentences.
- Select the negative word that is the opposite of the English indefinite word.
- Restructure the English sentence using *not* + the negative word chosen above.
- Fill in the negative phrase in the Spanish sentence.

1. I'm not going to do that ever.

   NEGATIVE WORD/PHRASE:_____

   RESTRUCTURE:_____

   No voy a hacer eso _____.

2. John isn't going to the party either.

   NEGATIVE WORD/PHRASE:_____

   RESTRUCTURE:_____

   Juan no va a la fiesta _____.

3. We don't have anything to do.

NEGATIVE WORD/PHRASE:_____

RESTRUCTURE:_____

No tenemos _____ que hacer.

4. They don't know anyone in Bogotá.

NEGATIVE WORD/PHRASE:_____

RESTRUCTURE:_____

No conocen a _____ en Bogotá.

STUDY TIPS — INDEFINITES AND NEGATIVES

Pattern (see *Tips for Learning Vocabulary,* pp. 1-3)

Learn the Spanish indefinites and negatives as pairs of opposites using the chart on p. 197. Notice the following similarities.

- the initial letters for many indefinites is **alg-**
- the initial letter for many negatives is **n-**

Flashcards

Create a flashcard for each of the indefinite and negative words.

algo	*something*
nunca	*never*

Practice

1. Sort out the negative cards and look at the English side. Provide the English indefinite word that is the opposite of the negative word on the card.

never	*sometimes*
none	*some, any*

2. Sort out the indefinite cards and look at the English side. Provide the English negative word that is the opposite of the negative word on the card.

something	*nothing*
someone	*no one, nobody*

3. Repeat steps 1 and 2 referring to the Spanish side of the cards.

4. Write (on a blank sheet of paper) affirmative Spanish sentences with indefinites. Then write the negative of those affirmative sentences.

Vi a **alguien** en el café.	*I saw **someone** in the café.*
No vi a **nadie** en el café.	*I didn't see **anyone** in the café.*

2. What is a Noun? 1. students, classroom, teacher 2. Wilsons, tour, Mexico 3. figure skating, event, Winter Olympics 4. Buenos Aires, capital, Argentina, city 5. truth, fiction 6. boss, intelligence, sense, humor

3. What is Meant by Gender? 1. M 2. ? 3. F 4. ? 5. ? 6. F 7. ?

4. What is Meant by Number? 1. P 2. S 3. S 4. P 5. P 6. S

5. What are Articles? 1. los 2. una 3. unas 4. el 5. un 6. las 7. unos 8. una 9. la

6. What is the Possessive? 1. the parents of some children 2. the office of the doctor 3. the headlights of a car 4. the soccer coach of the girls 5. the mother of Gloria Smith

7. What is a Verb? 1. purchase 2. were 3. enjoyed, preferred 4. ate, finished, went 5. was, to see, struggle, to get 6. attended, to celebrate

8. What is the Infinitive? 1. to do 2. study 3. to learn 4. leave 5. to travel

9. What is a Subject? 1. Q: What rang? A: The bell. (S) Q: Who ran out? A: The children. (P) 2. Q: Who took the order? A: One waiter. (S) Q: Who brought the food? A: Another. (S) 3. Q: Who voted? A: The first-year students (or The students) (P) 4. Q: Who says? A: They. (P) Q: What is a beautiful language? A: Spanish. (S)

10. What is a Pronoun? The antecedent is between parentheses. 1. she (Mary); him (Peter) 2. they (coat, dress) 3. herself (Isabel) 4. we (Robert, I) 5. it (book)

11. What is a Subject Pronoun? A. 1. 1st person, singular → yo 2. 3rd person, singular → 0 3. 1st person, plural → nosotros *or* nosotras 4. 3rd person, plural → 0 5. 3rd person, singular → él 6. 3rd person, plural → ellas B. 1. ustedes/ustedes 2. tú/tú 3. usted/usted 4. vosotros/ustedes 5. tú/tú 6. usted/usted

12. What is a Verb Conjugation? STEM: compr- CONJUGATION: yo compro; tú compras; él/ella/Ud. compra; nosotros compramos; vosotros compráis; ellos/ellas/Uds. compran

13. What are Auxiliary Verbs? English auxiliaries not used as auxiliaries in Spanish are in *italics*. 1. *will* 2. "are" is a Spanish auxiliary and is expressed with **estar** 3. *did* 4. "had" is a Spanish auxiliary and is expressed with **haber** 5. *do*

14. What are Affirmative and Negative Sentences? Words that indicate the negative are in *italics*. These italicized words are the same words that would not appear in the Spanish negative sentence. 1. We *do not (don't)* want to leave class early. 2. He *did not (didn't)* do his homework yesterday. 3. Teresa *will not (won't)* go to Chile this summer. 4. Robert *cannot (can't)* go to the restaurant with us.

15. What are Declarative and Interrogative Sentences? Words that indicate the interrogative are in *italics*. These italicized words are the same words that would not appear in the Spanish negative sentence. A. 1. *Did* Richard and Kathy study all evening? 2. *Does* your brother eat a lot? 3. *Do* the girl's parents speak Spanish? B. 1. My mother and father went to the movies, didn't they?

16. What are Some Equivalents of "to be"? A. 1. CH → ser 2. CO → estar 3. CO → estar 4. CH → ser 5. CO → estar 6. CO → estar 7. CH → ser B. 1. L → estar 2. P → hay 3. L → estar 4. P → hay

18. What is the Present Tense? 1. reads 2. is reading → lce 3. does read → lee 4. is reading → lee

19. What is the Past Tense? IMPERFECT: was, was checking, was handling, was crying, was, was leaving PRETERITE: went, arrived, ran, dropped, tried, ducked, grabbed, brought, comforted, smiled, boarded

20. What is a Participle? 1. P 2. PP 3. PP 4. P

21. What are the Progressive Tenses? 1. P 2. PG 3. PG 4. P 5. P

23. What is the Subjunctive? 1. S 2. S 3. I 4. S 5. S 6. S 7. I

24. What is the Imperative? A. 1. Study for the exam. 2. Let's go to the movies every weekend. 3. Eat more fruit and vegetables. B. 1. Don't sleep in class. 2. Don't work so much. 3. Let's not eat out tonight.

25. What are the Perfect Tenses? 1. had gone, PP 2. has left, P 3. will have graduated, FP 4. would have studied, CP; had remembered, PP 5. have seen, P

26. What is the Future Tense? 1. will study, study 2. 'll (will) clean, clean 3. shall leave, leave 4. won't (will not) finish, finish 5. will be, be

27. What is the Conditional? 1. P, F 2. C, IS 3. C or IS 4. P, F 5. PT, C 6. PS, CP

28. What is Meant by Active and Passive Voice? 1. cow, cow, Ac, PP 2. bill, Bob's parents Pa, PP 3. bank, bank, Ac, P 4. everyone, everyone, Ac, F 5. spring break, all, Pa, F

30. What is a Descriptive Adjective? The noun or pronoun described is between parentheses. 1. young (man), Spanish (newspaper) 2. pretty (she), new (dress), red (dress) 3. interesting (it) 4. old (piano), good (music) 5. tired (Paul), long (walk)

31. What is Meant by Comparison of Adjectives? The noun modified is between parentheses. 1. older (teacher), C+ 2. less intelligent (he), C- 3. as tall as (Mary), C= 4. the worst (boy), S 5. better (student), C+

32. What is a Possessive Adjective? The noun possessed is between parentheses. 1. my (book), S → mi 2. your (boots), P → tus 3. his (mother), S → su 4. our (children), P → nuestros

33. What is an Interrogative Adjective? A. The noun modified is between parentheses. 1. which (book) 2. what (exercises) 3. which (house) B. The noun modified is between parentheses. 1. how many (shirts), P → Cuántas 2. how much (wine), S → Cuánto 3. how many (telephones), P → Cuántos 4. how much (salad), S → Cuánta

34. What is a Demonstrative Adjective? The noun modified is between parentheses. 1. that (restaurant), S → ese 2. those (houses), P → Aquellas 3. these (shoes), P → estos 4. this (magazine), S → esta

35. What is an Adverb? The word modified is between parentheses. 1. early (arrived) 2. really (quickly), quickly (learned) 3. too (tired) 4. reasonably (secure) 5. very (well), well (speaks)

36. What is a Conjunction? The words to be circled are in *italics*; the words to be underlined are plain. 1. Mary *and* Paul; French *or* Spanish 2. She did not study *because* she was too tired. 3. Not only had he forgotten his ticket, *but* he had forgotten his passport as well.

37. What is a Preposition? 1. toward, of 2. from 3. around 4. at 5. between

38. What are Objects? 1. Q: The children took what? A: A shower → DO 2. Q: They ate what? A: The meal → DO Q: They

ate with whom? A: With their friends → OP 3. Q: He sent
what? A: A present → DO Q: He sent a present to whom?
A: To his brother → IO

39. What is an Object Pronoun? The words to be underlined are
in parentheses. 1. (it) DO, DO, book, S → lo 2. (them) DO,
DO, magazines, P → las 3. (them) IO, IO, P, U → les 4.
(him) IO, IO, S, M → le

40. What are Object of Preposition Pronouns? 1. them, P, F →
ellas 2. her, S, F → ella 3. you, S, NA → ti 4. us, P, NA →
nosotros or nosotras

41. What are Reflexive Pronouns and Verbs? A. 1. herself → se
2. yourself → te 3. ourselves → nos 4. themselves → se
B. 1. each other, RP 2. themselves, RX 3. each other, RP
4. myself, RX 5. each other RP

42. What is a Possessive Pronoun? The antecedent is between
parentheses. 1. mine (car), S → el mío 2. hers (parents), P
→ los suyos 3. yours (boots), P → Las tuyas 4. ours (bicycle), S → la nuestra

43. What is an Interrogative Pronoun? A. The words to be
underlined are in parentheses. 1. (Whose) P, Of whom is
the sweater → De quién 2. (who), O, To whom are you
talking → quién 3. (who), S → Quiénes

44. What is a Demonstrative Pronoun? The antecedent is
between parentheses. 1. this one (dress), NS, S → éste
2. that one (notebook), NPS, S → Ése 3. those over there
(houses), A, P → aquéllas

45. What is a Relative Pronoun? The words to be circled are
between parentheses. 1. that (letter), DO → que 2. who
(woman), S → que 3. Paul is the student with whom I
traveled. whom (student), OP → quien 4. what (NA), S →
lo que

46. What are Indefinites and Negatives? The words to be underlined are between parentheses. 1. (ever) never; I'm not
going to do that never → nunca 2. (either) neither; John
isn't going to the party neither → tampoco 3. (anything),
nothing; we don't have nothing to do → nada
4. (anyone), no one; they don't know no one in Bogotá →
nadie